PRAISE FOR THE AUTHOR

I enthusiastically endorse Glen Michaelides for his Business Coaching and Personal Mentoring. Glen was able to identify some strategic Competitive advantages we were able to apply to our High Profile Power Fitness Gymnasium, to up our membership extensively. Glen left no stone unturned with his approach in ensuring we had a real rubber-to-the-road plan. I can assure you that working with Glen will produce positive results.

**Peta and Adam Baker,
'Bodybuilding Champions' Power Fitness, Perth WA**

For more than a decade we have worked alongside Glen… Always trying something new, and a more innovative thinker we are yet to meet. Staying ahead of the competition takes skill, perseverance, and commitment to ensure the best results. Thinking out of the box can often be the difference to success and failure and in these times a 'must have' characteristic. We are proud to have him as a business associate and, equally importantly, a good friend.

Mark and Karen Oliver Directors RV Trade and Fleet P/L

Honesty, Integrity and Trust Are Currency in today's Turbulent Economy

Our industry and clients demand a supremely high level of customer service and support. Over the last nine years Glen has delivered high quality solutions

Doing what it takes to get it right the first time and going the extra mile to get to the desired result for our clients – I would have no hesitation in recommending Glen for leveraging your business results.

Steve Senior, Fleet Manager, Grand Toyota

I would urge anyone serious about improving their business to read this book. I have watched Glen overcome obstacles in business that most people would buckle under, and – more than overcome – go on to thrive from the challenge and create bigger and better results in his company.

Ian Marsh, CEO Streetsmart Business School

It was clear from the beginning that Glen was true to his word

Over the last 15 years, Glen has been true to his word and created action to make an immediate difference. His organised approach to getting what's important done is the difference between success and failure. I strongly endorse Glen and look forward too many more high quality results.

Kelvin Mansfield, Flexi.com.au

The divine universe works in mysterious ways. They say when the student soul is ready the master soul teacher will appear. Well I met Glen in high altitude, in mid-air, on a plane. Since that day, I have been divinely assigned to work with Glen to awaken his inner journey to expand as an energy alignment master. I've witnessed Glen work his magic by transforming energy to align with a higher vibration to receive change at a quantum speed. This book is infinitely charged with this energy so get ready to feel and receive this! An energy alignment transformation with Glen awaits you, to expand your business and life from the inside out. Namaste!

**Diane Rawiri, Energy Alignment Master,
Business & Life Transformation Coach/Consultant,
Director of Xseelence Pty Ltd & Weaving Miracles**

TAKE YOUR
BUSINESS TO THE
NEXT LEVEL

GLOBAL
PUBLISHING
G R O U P

Global Publishing Group
Australia • New Zealand • Singapore • America • London

TAKE YOUR BUSINESS TO THE NEXT LEVEL

The Essential Guide to Transforming your Business and Profits in Today's Economy

$2,997
FREE
Business
Building
Tools

Glen Michaelides

First Edition 2016

National Library of Australia
Cataloguing-in-Publication entry:

Creator: Michaelides, Glen, author.

Title: Take Your Business to the Next Level : The Essential Guide to Transforming Your Business and Profits in Today's Economy / Glen Michaelides

1st ed.
ISBN: 9781925288292 (paperback)

Organizational change
Corporate profits
Success in business

Dewey Number: 658.406

Published by Global Publishing Group
PO Box 517 Mt Evelyn, Victoria 3796 Australia
Email info@GlobalPublishingGroup.com.au

Printed in China

For further information about orders:
Phone: +61 3 9739 4686 or Fax +61 3 8648 6871

This Book is dedicated to My Outstanding Wife and Children.

Who have ridden the entrepreneurial roller-coaster with me through the challenges of Business and life.

Never wavering in their unconditional love and support. Giving me the energy, strength and confidence to carry on through my most challenging times to realise my full potential.

And for them and with the grace of God I will be forever grateful.

Glen Michaelides

ACKNOWLEDGEMENTS

I have been lucky enough to have encountered many great experiences in my life to date.

The ups, the downs, the painful times and the euphoric moments, such as watching my children brought into the world, and marriage to my beautiful wife.

I am Truly Grateful for all of the opportunity's presented for me and the spectrum of emotions felt deep within my core.

To my Parents, who always did their level best to instil in me high quality Morals, Values and Ethics and who continue to be a guiding light in my daily ability and willingness to help others achieve their goals.

A Special Thank You to the many Mentors that have helped guide me along my path.

Tony Robbins, Darren Stephens, Dr Richard Bandler, Robin Sharma, Diane Rawiri, Robert Kiyosaki, Michael Gerber, Mal Emery, Ian Marsh, Napoleon Hill, Arnold Schwarzenegger and Stephen Covey, to name a few. Willing to share their wisdom through books, seminars and coaching. Leaving their personal mark on my effectiveness to create Outstanding results for myself and others.

To my Valued Clients of who in helping has exited the power and motivation to continue my lifelong ambition to create High Quality Value and inspiration for those searching and in need.

FREE Bonus Offers

Fast Track Success Academy

Valued at $2,997 – Yours FREE!

The Package includes:

- **Module 1** – Designing your Ultimate Life
- **Module 2** – Mastering your mindset for prosperity
- **Module 3** – 7 ways to Increase customers
- **Module 4** – 5 ways to generate more income
- **Module 5** – How to increase your Profits effectively
- **Module 6** – Building and keeping the Ultimate Team

Valued at $2,997 – Yours FREE!

To Download go to:
http://thetitansacademy.com/index.php?/register/lAf38gfe

CONTENTS

FOREWORD
by Mal Emery

Glen Michaelides is a VERY rare breed and an even rarer commodity and I am completely and utterly qualified to make that statement.

I am often asked, but I rarely do forewords for books. In Glen's case, I am making a rare exception, simply because if I impress upon you how talented and skilful Glen really is, then there is a better than reasonable chance that you will do something that most people who buy books never do and that is read the damn thing.

You see, I know firsthand how talented Glen is and how capable he is at helping you in your business. I say that because I have firsthand knowledge of him transforming an ordinary business to an extraordinary business – TWICE.

How come twice you might ask?

Well through no fault of Glen's, his business was literally destroyed by the downturn in the mining industry. By the way, he wasn't alone in that either.

When Glen's business got wiped out he was top dog of his industry, which he built from humble beginnings to complete and utter domination of his category. Even then, that wasn't enough to survive what happened to the mining industry.

But what I saw next was nothing short of amazing… Even though I am sure Glen went through his own share of sleepless nights wondering what to do.

But I bet there wasn't too many sleepless nights because Glen grabbed this monster by the scruff of its neck, repositioned and rejigged his business to be no longer dependent on the mining industry.

After all, it was reinvention or oblivion anyway.

And of course, now he has done it again. He is now dominating his new category.

That is not how most people handle disasters. Most people curl up in the corner timidly doing nothing when such obstacles strike.

I will tell you now, if I was going to war and let's face is, business today is a war, I would want Glen Michaelides on my side.

One last thing…

There are a lot of so-called experts that write books on various subjects. Mostly they have not actually done what they are writing about, mostly their books are based on research and study and not the real world.

Glen's book is not one of these… Glen has actually done what he is teaching you here and even more importantly, he is still doing it today, so he knows better than most what it is like to walk in your moccasins.

If you are reading this with a view to putting your hand in your pocket and purchasing this book, I suggest you do, in fact, I highly recommend it.

If you are reading it based on already making a purchase, then you will be very glad you did.

INTRODUCTION

"A big heartfelt Thank You" for taking an interest and time in investing in yourself. I don't believe there is anything more gratifying than improving one's knowledge towards a more prosperous lifestyle for you, and for all you come in contact with.

What is the Next Level? Interesting question – understanding that you have picked up this book tells me you are searching for something. Even though I don't know you personally I do understand you have taken action investing in this book, so it is more than likely you are looking for one of the following;

More money, more time, more success, maybe even better health or possibly outstanding relationships with family and friends.

My hunch is it could be all of the above so, the 'Next Level' is a personal quest that **only you** can put a limit on. Whatever your dreams and ambitions are the fact is you would not dream them if you were not capable of achieving them.

In this book I will be sharing my own real life rubber-to-the-road strategies, and the tools I have used to build multimillion dollar businesses for myself and many others.

Most importantly you have made a decision to move towards what you desire and move away from what you don't.

The road can be more difficult at times, and one less travelled, but stay on the path and ignore the killjoys as the rewards are worth it.

I truly commend you for being one of brave few strong enough to stand up as a leader, step up to the plate of life, and give it everything you have.

THE STORM IS COMING – ARE YOU READY?

CHAPTER 1

THE STORM IS COMING – ARE YOU READY?

What if I was to tell you that, on its own, *Taking Your Business to The Next Level* could be a sure-fire way to disaster?

More than likely you would be a little confused due to the title of this book.

I want you to read the words, listen with your ears, but most importantly I want you to hear with your heart.

As only this will keep you on your true course, even when the storm comes from out of nowhere and blows the world as you know it upside down.

If you don't know what I'm talking about, it may not be too late for you to make a real difference before things get interesting, and minimise the damage now.

If you do know what I'm talking about, know that there is growth and wisdom in your struggles, as for you – the action-taker – there will always be options to rebuild and get back on top.

There is a reason you have picked up this book. You were guided, as within these pages you will discover the strategies, tools and psychology that, if followed, will indeed set in motion the potential for you to become extremely successful.

Years in the trenches doing it the Hard Way, and then an Easier Way, has taught me incredible lessons.

You get to leverage off if you choose, and potentially minimise the heartache and costly mistakes for yourself along the way.

If taking your *business* to the Next Level is the only reason you picked up this book I would suggest you put it back down.

However, if you're up for building the internal fortitude required to sustain yourself and keep reaching your Next Levels then read on.

As it is this internal strength, not external support, that will allow you to weather the turbulent conditions known as business and life. Importantly – keeping you climbing when the going gets tuff.

This is your oxygen when you are at altitude, and will stop you from getting the sickness that sometimes comes with the climb.

You may be surprised to learn *Taking Your Business to The Next Level* is almost always opposite of what most think.

If you look at any master in their field you typically only see 'the result'; we are almost hypnotised by what they have become, their almost superhuman status. Sporting personalities, business icons, rock stars, or top performers of any kind. But if you dig deeper you will invariably find a long disciplined road to greatness.

While others are horsing around, or watching five hours of TV a day, the masters in their fields are studying, practising, and honing their craft, using methods seldom talked about, to become the best in their chosen field.

You will get the chance to learn some of these methods in future chapters.

FAIR WARNING THOUGH – THESE METHODS HAVE BEEN KNOWN TO CAUSE SIDE EFFECTS SUCH AS PASSION, WEALTH, HAPPINESS AND SUCCESS.

There is also a good chance it will be a challenge for you to think they have not come straight out of the pages of a science fiction novel.

The choices for you are simple, either stay in a hypnotised coma-like state and keep surrounding yourself with the people who agree with the same story. Or break free from the make-believe and find the real you, the one you have been hiding underneath all of the layers of conditioning, lies and ego.

You may not quite know what the journey is right now. Don't worry, your heart and soul know, and they will guide you in the direction you need to travel.

You may have felt this movement inside of you from an early age, a force that you could not quite put your finger on. But it is strong and guiding you always forever forward, this inner knowing that you are meant for more something bigger.

Don't ignore this, as not everyone has it, you are the chosen one that is gifted to give more than the average person can. You, my friend, are far from average and have the power to change the world in your unique way.

So it is here, my fellow Titan, where you get to decide whether to keep lying to yourself or step up and take the position that is rightfully yours. The one you were built for.

The Lessons of Complacency

I can remember thinking to myself, how am I going to fit this fat wallet full of cash in my pocket? I was looking at it almost as if it was an inconvenience and thinking how uncomfortable it would be to walk around all day with a fat bulging pocket.

Of course, this was ridiculous, and I realised not long after how arrogant and stupid I was. At the time I was invincible and could not do a thing wrong, almost like I was Teflon-coated, nothing would stick to me, except the money that kept rolling in.

How did I forget so soon where I had come from? From looking under the couch cushions and the seats of my car for loose change to buy a loaf of bread. To having enough money to live comfortably and buy most things I wanted.

The quicker I spent it, the faster I would make more, and fill up my bank accounts or buy something new to keep the excitement and lies alive.

The years of sacrifice had finally paid off, or so I thought, and there I was standing at the top of the mountain I had been climbing for over 20 years. Full of bravado for what I had achieved.

Multimillion dollar homes, boats, exotic cars, holidays to locations around the world. The stuff of dreams for most of us right? The trophies we chase to try and fill a never-ending unquenchable thirst.

Don't get me wrong, it did not come easy, I did it the hard way, there was some serious blood, sweat and tears shed along the way. So there I was, an overnight success after 20 years of hard work.

How did I feel after achieving all of that success? The truth is, not like I thought I would. Not the level of happiness I had assumed anyway.

Why may you ask? Because I did not realise how important the **Journey** really was.

I never took the time to build up the internal fortitude required to deal with success – or failure for that matter.

I was running too fast to realise that success does not exist trying to bask in the glory at your Next Level, **more in the space in between**.

That, at times, very uncomfortable place where you are required to give and be more, not acting from programming, fear or scarcity.

More from trust and abundance, in spite of the uncertainty and at times crazy things that happen on the journey.

So why was I reacting all of the time, running at an unsustainable pace, trying to control every outcome, wanting to fix everything myself and not give others a chance, as I felt they would more than likely stuff it up?

I was blinded by the dependency of an Urgency Addiction, not happy unless there was too much to do, and I was running hard to put the fires out and be the hero that saved the day.

My motivation was the fear and scarcity of not having enough; a tough, relentless master, hell-bent on driving you into the ground.

I did not understand what I did not know then, as time had to offer up the lessons first for me to reach a much calmer, wiser, more measured version of my former self.

Don't get me wrong I still have two jet turbines for engines that I can fire up at will.

The difference is *I* decide when to fire them up and create massive action, not my circumstances, and I certainly don't use them to put heat on people as I did in the past. As I mentioned before you get to leverage my hindsight.

When Will I Be Happy?

When I pay my house off I will be happy; as soon as I can afford to buy a new, more powerful car I will be happy. If I can get to a million and then two million dollars in my bank account, then I will celebrate.

The truth is that happiness never happened to me, as I never took the time to really think about it. I had not realised that happiness was up to me and came from inside, not outside, so the more I ticked the boxes, the more I went after, and the more I took things for granted.

Not to mention the trail of unhappiness I left behind me; here I was saying I was making all of this money and buying all of the stuff for my wife and kids to give them a better life. Honestly, to a large part that was all lies, I was doing it for myself to satisfy my wants, fears and desires, and to keep fuelling the big ego I had created, and that had gotten out of control.

The emptiness of having achieved all of the material things felt like a Black Hole inside that I could never fill – the more you get, the more you try and fill the void that can never be filled, and so the cycle repeats.

In fact, I felt more fear and scarcity after I had achieved what I thought was the success than I had ever felt when I had no money.

There is nowhere to hide from the fear, lack and want, as the deepest harm and terrorism often exists inside our mind, and not outside, like we think or blame.

Please don't misunderstand me as there is a dichotomy here – I am very much an advocate of having bountiful things, and I believe you should look forward to having the luxuries in life. And I really want that for you.

It is only when all the things control and dominate your decisions, leaving no room for what really matters that it becomes a problem.

Ask yourself this question and think about this carefully "Do you think and take action on *what really matters to you the most* first – or is it distant second?"

The Gift of Not Getting

You see I'm not one of these people who was born with a silver spoon in my mouth, I come from very humble beginnings.

Never going without the basics as a child; we always had enough to eat, a roof over our heads and all of the general items you need to get by.

My parents – good, honest law-abiding citizens – instilled strong values deep within my core. Honesty, integrity and commitment, guiding me on my mission to this day, lessons I am truly thankful for.

As far as extras and the latest mod-cons went well, there was not a lot left over for that. That did not stop me wanting them though.

Thinking back to my childhood, I did not know I was going to be an entrepreneur and a business person. The unusual turn of events in life is not planned or orchestrated, more forged out of circumstances and, at times, hardships and misfortunes.

I was the black sheep of the family, growing up in a very conservative house, my parents, who I love dearly, doing the best they knew how from what they were taught.

Unknown to them they spoke a language of fear and scarcity to get compliance and try and make me conform to what society wanted me to be. Not for any malicious reasons, purely from wanting the best for me in the only way they knew how.

The neighbourhood I grew up in was quite rough and challenging at times. You became street savvy at an early age; I would often be on the lookout to evade the local bullies, out to cause trouble, and who were all too willing to handing out beatings for the fun of it. I did not want to be on the receiving end as it was never a fair fight.

Thinking back, the only exposure I had to wealthy people was my godparents. We rarely saw them, maybe once every couple of years when we would go to their mansion to spend the day.

I think my parents chose them because they were wealthy, not because we were close. I don't believe they realised the profound effect this would have, as it has stayed with me all my lifetime. Their lavish house was on the river with the best views and had everything you could imagine. All of this for an eight-year-old – it was an adventure, to say the least.

A huge below-ground swimming pool with a built in spa and a real-life diving board. Brand new sports car in the driveway. Quite impressive in 1980. No one else we knew lived like this, particularly where I was from.

Apart from the house and cars, they owned a thriving restaurant in the local area, and it was here that I joined the dots as to why they were different than we were. The connection in my mind was that owning a business equalled big houses, nice things and all of the stuff I did not have, and now wanted.

What a stark contrast from where we lived, and honestly I would never have known what we did not have, in a monetary sense, if I had not seen it with my own eyes. The problem was I did see it, and I would often ask my parents *why do they own a business and live in that mansion, and we don't?*

I would never get a straight answer to that question – thinking back, I may have somewhat insulted my parents by asking it.

I eventually stopped asking them, but continued to ask myself the same question, which has stayed with me for the longest time. The 24-carat gold necklace with Saint Christopher my godparents brought for me as a birthday present is a reminder that I still have today.

So what's your epiphany moment? Think back to the earliest memory you have, what has been the spark for your life to driving you to this point?

Good bad or otherwise it does not matter – what started it all for you?

Tough Love

I would often be asking my parents for something that there was clearly no money for. That, more often than, not earnt me the Wooden Spoon. For those who don't know what a Wooden Spoon is, let's just say it was the tool of choice back in the day for getting urgent compliance.

Little did I realise at the time my Mum in her 'tough love' kind of a way, taught me the first rule of entrepreneurship: if you want something bad enough "Get up and go and get it for yourself".

This fired me up to learn ingenious ways of earning an income at an early age. From collecting Cool Drink bottles, to working underage in factories, sweeping the floors and shredding paper.

I can remember working in a factory that distributed high-end crystal products; my job was to shred the paper so the line-workers could pack the boxes for the outward freight. On occasions, I would get a glimpse of the owner of the company walking through the factory floor, always with a look of purpose and grace. A well-dressed man, with perfectly crafted grey hair and a sense of undoubtable quality and respect about him.

I would often think of myself as an owner of my company and how it would look and feel to be rich and successful.

Not a straight-A student, I was told at school the best job I could hope for was a mechanic or a tradesman of some description. When I set my mind to it I could get good grades, but frankly, I thought school for the large part was boring and frustrating. All I could think of was, "When am I going to learn what my godparents knew about business and how to become wealthy".

My lack of grades made way for street smarts, and a good brain when it came to solving problems creatively. I would often distract the class and wind up in trouble on a daily basis, earning me the privilege of putting away the chairs at the end of the day – I think mostly because of my smart, quick-witted answering back to the teacher when I was challenged.

I knew this was frustrating, as my boisterous nature would often embarrass them in front of the class. You might know what I'm talking about here as entrepreneurs in the making can be lousy students, and employees for that matter. Often giving their teacher or employer glimpses of high intelligence, and the hope that they could or would conform and provide leverage for their class or business. To blaze their trail and further frustrate, going from excellent performance and creative ideas one day, to complete disobedience the next.

Teachers and managers are seldom taught the skills in how to harness and focus the energy and power of creative thinkers, who are seen more like distractions, troublemakers and are often put in the too-hard basket.

Isn't it interesting though how powerful a suggestion can be at any age, especially to young people?

I ended up becoming a mechanic, resigned to the fact that was my place because of average school grades. I hated almost every minute of it. Like any teenage boy I loved cars, but I did not want to work on them, especially in very hot, dirty and average conditions

I would often get annoyed by stigma that was attached to tradespeople and their supposed lack of intelligence, and at times that got me down.

The paradox of all this was my firmly installed value of Never Giving Up left me completing the apprenticeship, gritting my teeth the whole way through. Don't get me wrong I don't think doing an apprenticeship or a trade of any kind is a bad thing on the contrary, it taught me valuable skills and lessons I use to this day.

The point I am making is you have a choice to do whatever your passionate about, it's never too late so if you're not happy keep searching and don't let anyone tell you otherwise.

I had forgotten about my godparents and their sports car and house on the river. But I think somewhere deep inside the memory sat, poking me in the ribs, asking me to move forward and *let go of the things I was good at, to go after the things I would be great at.*

I was an average mechanic, only good enough to get by. Where I did excel was in the interaction with the clients, talking about their vehicle and upselling them on extras and add-ons. This was a part of the job I did enjoy, and I think I made more for the company in sales than I did in revenue from twisting spanners.

I have to admit the other enjoyable part was taking exotic cars for test drives. Certainly was a lot of fun, especially for an 18-year-old.

I would often swing by my mate's house and showboat for a bit before heading back to work.

Finding my feet

When the company suddenly closed down, I was left without a job.

Almost immediately from out of nowhere a new opportunity opened up for me in a sales position within my industry.

I was using something very powerful, that at the time I was unaware of. As mentioned we will go deeper into this phenomenon in upcoming chapters as the power is limited only by the user.

A dedicated sales role was exactly what I wanted, and it was a smooth and natural transition for me, as I already had the product knowledge, coupled with an ability to solve complex problems and build relationships quickly.

It turns out this was a winning formula, which soon, at age 21, made me a top performer of the company. I went on to successfully manage two branches, all within the space of a year.

I tried to grow a moustache in the effort to look older, only really succeeding in looking more like some 80s porn star instead. I thought it was pretty cool at the time and anyway, I was managing people 30 years my senior, so I tried to look older. I thought they would not feel so bad about themselves if I didn't remind them I was only 21 and they were 50 and doing the same thing they started on.

Thankfully I grew out of that phase, but I still can't escape some of the photos my wife took at the time, bringing them out at inappropriate times for a laugh.

With my moustache days over, it was not long until the word got around that I was a must have, resulting in many phone calls from competitors all wanting me to work for them. I could not help myself, more money, a better company vehicle and all the perks… well my ego was exploding so I had to take the best offer, of course.

Young and worldly-inexperienced I was only looking at the benefits and fast-tracking to my goal of one day owning my own business, and all of the success and wealth that I figured came with it.

So I was willingly 'poached' out of that company, as we called it. Lucky for my new employer, as I went on to build two multimillion dollar businesses respectively from the ground up. And I worked bloody hard doing it.

Married to my wife at 22 and with our first child on the way – the owner of the company in his moment of generosity gave me two days off for the birth. So much for all of the perks, as this was not up for negotiation. I was the front man so I had to be there manning the fort and making him a fortune while he jetted around the country.

I regretted this experience, and my wife suffered as a young mum through this time without me being there. As I mentioned earlier I was young, inexperienced and hell-bent on becoming a successful business owner.

So what would my current-age version of myself do in this situation? Well, let me ask this question again, "Do you put the most important things first? Or are they a distant second?"

As I mentioned, entrepreneurs don't make good employees and eventually I felt under-remunerated for my efforts, and taken for granted, so I was going to walk out the door.

What happens next? Well, keep reading because it's about to get interesting.

CHAPTER 2

RUN AS FAST AS YOU CAN

CHAPTER 2

RUN AS FAST AS YOU CAN

With your foot flat on the gas all of the time there's a good chance you will blow the motor.

It turns out I did not actually leave after all. Before I had an opportunity to hand in my notice and throw five years of effort away, I was turned around at the door.

I think the boss had a sixth sense for what I was about to do – I was about to leave all of my efforts behind to someone who in my mind did not deserve it.

Why did he not deserve it? Well, there was a promise made to me – my job was to build a company from scratch to an agreed value. Once that had been achieved the deal was to sell the company and I would be gifted a portion of the business.

Fair deal, he put up the capital and risk, and I made it happen, only now he had changed his mind, as things were going well, and he was making good money with little input or effort. When I reminded him of the deal, he said no, the timing is not right; I think we will wait.

So here I was with five years invested, and with my eye on the prize to raise enough capital to buy my own business. The problem was I never had it put into writing and drawn up legally from the start, assuming everyone had the same strong value system as me and that trust was high on the list.

Always cover yourself and your IP upfront as this will avoid painful experiences down the track. Sounds elementary, but failure to do so can devastate you overnight.

I asked him many times, but the answer was always vague, like "Yes we will get to that, should not be a problem, I'm just tied up at the moment".

As you can guess that went on and on and eventually I stopped asking, as clearly he wanted his cake and to eat it too. But I kept thinking to myself how many times am I going to make other people wealthy and how many years was I going to continue wasting doing it?

I was called into the office, waiting for what I thought was going to be an interrogation session on why I was leaving and so on. I think the owner of the company realised what he was potentially losing, and that was going to be a lot more than just me, as I had the relationship with the clients and it was strong – so strong all of them would have followed me in a heartbeat.

How do I know this? Because they were also my friends. You see I understood very early that a return on the relationship was far more important than a return on investment.

I would go the extra mile and provide massive value long before I expected a return: *if you have your eye only on yourself or your profits only, you will get a ring seat view of yourself and your profits diminishing in value, quicker than you think.*

So there I was standing in his office, and he said: "Glen, we are going to sell the business, and I'm going to make good on my offer and give you the money".

I nearly dropped down to one knee as the excitement was overwhelming, he was making good, this was going to happen. It turns out though, not exactly the way I thought it would.

You see life has an interesting sense of humour as he said to me, "Yes I'm going to sell you the business, and you can buy it off me for the price, less your cut".

As you can imagine I was on a roller-coaster of emotion, as I had the money for 30 seconds and now it had been taken away. How was I going to come up with the substantial balance?

I said, "How am I supposed to pay you?" I had some money saved up but nowhere near the amount needed to pay the value of the business.

He said you could pay it off, I did not stop and think about it or ask too many questions, I just said yes and then started running.

I had run hard before – the day I got my licence my Mother had dropped me down at the licensing centre to do the test. I felt like I always had an affinity with motor vehicles so getting my licence was easy, and I passed the first attempt.

As we got back into the car and started to drive off, she said to me, "Don't be ungrateful, express your thanks for me dropping you off". I said back to her, "Well I did all the work, I was the one that passed the test".

I don't remember how fast the car was going, but she managed to lean over open the door and push a six-foot, 85 kg teenager out of it while it was still coming to a stop. Still not exactly sure how she did that, maybe

I partially assisted as I still remember the look on her face and how angry she was at me. Rightfully so, I was a real ungrateful so-and-so that day. I know that now, but at the time, after she drove off and left me 20 km from home, I had other thoughts going through my mind, as I had waited all of this time to get my licence.

My car was waiting for me at home in the driveway, I had been paying off and working on for the last year and a half, and now I had to find a way home…

I just started sprinting – as a football player I was definitely fit, it was not uncommon for me to run many kilometres in a game. But I was so angry she left me I just keep running as fast as I could. Strangely I did not seem to tire out, even after 20 km of running.

Part of me wanted to show her that it did not affect me and prove I did not need her help I could do It on my own. Also, I just wanted to drive my car for the first time and experience the freedom that came with that.

When I made it home in what seemed like only two hours, I could see she was surprised. With a look of almost how on earth did he get here so quick?

This was a valuable lesson that at the time I did not recognise.

Because something very profound happened to me that day – how was it I could run 20 km and it seemed like nothing? What was going on inside my brain and body for this to happen?

I would learn later how to harness the Power of this secret weapon, at the time though I did not pay too much attention to it. Not joining the dots as to why at times we can achieve difficult feats easily, and other times struggle to get out of bed in the morning.

So, after saying yes to buying the business, I just started running hard. Forgetting why I wanted to go into business in the first place.

I wanted the freedom to make my decisions, and create my style, ensuring trust, integrity and good old-fashioned service for the clients and employees alike.

And there I was, a business owner in all my glory; I did not think about the fact that I was paying so much money for a company I had built from the ground up.

It was an opportunity, and I was going for It. I had got what I wanted but not exactly in the way I wanted it.

The power of clarity

I want you to do this exercise – think back to anything significant you have achieved throughout your life. To achieve it in the first place you had to see it in your mind's eye and think about it with clarity.

How badly did you want it? Did it consume your every thought? And wake you up in the middle of the night thinking about it?

Did you see it as if it had already happened, and you were already living in the three-storey house enjoying a cold drink on the balcony overlooking the ocean, driving your dream car, or sailing your 40-foot boat on the sea?

What did it look like, did you hear the sounds of the waves crashing in and the seagulls in the distance, could you smell the new leather upholstery and feel the power of the engine? Whatever it is for you.

The clearer the picture – the more focused you get, the more energy you put behind it, the big enough 'why' you want it – the more accurately you will get what you want.

How does this work? Well this is where it gets interesting… You have built into your brain a secret weapon when it comes to achieving your desired results. It's called your Reticular Activating System, or RAS.

Now, you can deliberately **program** the RAS by choosing the exact messages you send from your conscious mind. This powerful system engages your brain kind of like a heat-seeking missile that will hunt down and find the intended target you have programmed it for.

Let me give you an example:

Have you ever experienced looking for and then buying a new car, to find all of a sudden you see them everywhere? As if a surprising number of people have just suddenly brought the same model at the same time?

How does this happen? This well-known and documented phenomenon is being driven by the RAS. This system cannot distinguish the difference between real events and imagined reality. Set it an outcome, get clarity and make it a must, and the RAS will step into action.

My RAS was primed and ready for action when I bought the business, so why was it not the way I thought it would be?

I believe that it wasn't for two reasons – life having a sense of humour and wanting me to grow and stretch myself, and me not being clear enough.

You see, I was just seeing and thinking of myself as a business owner, and not getting clear enough on the exact outcome I wanted.

Not realising it at the time but I did actually get exactly what I was asking for.

So think carefully about what you really want, be very specific to ensure your outcome is in line with what you're priming your RAS for.

Regardless of business not working out exactly the way I wanted, my hard efforts were really paying off. The business was going from strength to strength. As right or wrong I was running on sheer willpower and determination, concentrating on only getting results.

I thought to myself I must be the Ultimate Businessman; I believed it, and others told me so it must have been true. Here I was an average grade student, with A-grade students working for me, and I thought to myself doing well in business had nothing to do with my grades at school.

There definitely was an element of skill and craft I was honing as a business owner, although I needed to learn some new skills quickly to keep things under control, as the market was extremely buoyant.

The money started to flow and I mean flow, it was not long until I had made a serious dent in the massive debt I had taken on buying the business.

I enjoyed having the equity to pay all of my bills and buy some nice things including a new two-storey house. A five-car garage, with a car in each space, outdoor kitchen with a cedar roof huge below ground swimming pool with water fountains, the list goes on.

Do You Want to be Rich or Free?

What I didn't consider or understand is that there is a big difference between being rich, and being free.

I was far from free, working on average 65 to 70 hours-plus a week; I had the nice things but no time to enjoy them. Fourteen million-plus in revenue and 50 staff took some serious managing.

No matter who you talk to, everybody wants to be financially free, but most don't understand being rich has nothing to do with it. I was doing what it took to be rich, and at the same time, I was pushing my freedom further and further out of my reach.

So why did you get into business in the first place? I have a very strong hunch it's not because you wanted to have your freedom taken away. I would assume not in the long term anyway.

As we go through our day-to-day schedules of busyness, demands and the expectations that we have often unwittingly placed on ourselves, stopping long enough to take stock of thoughts is not typically high on most people's To-Do Lists. The carousel of life seems to be stuck on fast forward for most of us, as we only get time to touch quickly the bases, like a baseball player desperately trying to get to home before being struck out.

Try and be conscious to the consistent improvement of your thoughts, as this is certainly a worthy way of improving all areas of your life.

The truth is we become what we think about, and our subsequent actions are the result of our thoughts! Could it be that simple? If I apply controlled effort in consistently thinking and acting in a certain way, that is all I need to do to change my circumstances and invariably my life?

Do this simple exercise – take note and count, in a single hour, how many of your thoughts are positive and inspiring, moving towards your 'clear, concise goals for your life', or negative and 'moving away from what you want'. If we are the sum of our thinking, what affect do you think each Negative or Positive Thought will have in getting what you want?

'We can only be what we think.' All our life-circumstances are a direct result of our thoughts, as we are the only ones that can have our thoughts – so it would be fair to say we are the only ones responsible for where we are today.

Thoughts are like seeds, your mind does not know the difference between what you plant, so that is why you are here at the crossroads. Bad thoughts will invariably harvest an adverse outcome, as good thoughts will eventually harvest good outcomes.

Don't forget, even if you have the best intentions, if you are consistently sabotaging your results by thinking in a poor way you will undo all of your hard work, as most people don't think they are worthy and believe it, so they never make it.

It can make an exponential difference having something to aim for, as every step towards a worthwhile purpose is a move in the right direction, and you will start experiencing the benefits of every good thought in achieving your worthy ideal.

Stay strong as this action – thinking positive thoughts – is like building muscle that will eventually be steadfast in stamping out unwanted negative thoughts.

So, what had happened to my thoughts? As mentioned in Chapter 1, I had more fear and scarcity with all of the niceties in life than when I had nothing.

You see, I did not understand back then the affect my thinking was having on my business, health, relationships and eventually my bank accounts. The very power I used to build my wealth was starting to tear it down. If you have ever watched a multi-storey building being built, it takes the time. Floor upon floor and only in the fullness of time, maybe years can completion be reached.

Now, have you ever seen a multi-storey building be demolished in a matter of seconds? What took years to build comes crashing down. Cascading floor upon floor until all that is left is rubble and debris.

You see, I was doing some things right in my business, no doubt about it, but I was doing a lot wrong as well.

And I was being artificially propped up, carried along by the tailwinds of an unprecedented mining boom, the likes of which our country, in fact the world, had not seen before. It got to a point that It almost did not matter what you charged for a vehicle. As long as your quality, speed and delivery we at a high standard you got the job.

My company would project manage light vehicle build-ups so they were fit for purpose. With all of the correct safety products and enhancements so they could tackle the harsh Australian outback. The conditions in the north-west of Australia can be extreme, to say the least, 45 degree days of relentless sun, unforgiving terrain, flood-ways, wildlife, kangaroos, cattle and emus, all a daily hazard.

Not to mention the mine sites themselves, super pits so big that they can be seen from space. Rocky, rugged and highly corrugated roads that would go on for hundreds of kilometres.

That's not all we did. We also built up recreational 4WD vehicles for the owners to tour the country, or just to make the vehicles more capable and enhance their looks.

This part was a lot of fun, as I grew up camping and exploring my country, which was coupled with my love for vehicles. You could get out there and see some amazing sights and have a ball along the way.

During the peak of the mining boom, there was not a lot of time for that, as it was not uncommon to have at least 130-plus commercial vehicles on site waiting to come in and get worked on. Trucks would turn up with more vehicles daily, and we would sometimes have to turn them away as we had run out of room to hold anymore.

We were all running flat out, and my staff was showing the signs of fatigue. It became hard to hold on to good people. Back then, you had to pay exceptional money as the unemployment rate was almost non-existent and jobs were going unfilled.

This went on for years – the money was great, but the logistics and staff issues were at times very interesting to balance and to manage. We had expanded as far as I was prepared to go, with as many staff as I could handle dealing with, and our stock holding and infrastructure was at a scary size.

Now I had managed to handle the business during these times with only limited training apart from on the job knowhow, gut instinct, and willpower.

Murmurs of China slowing down were starting to gain momentum, and other countries were seeing some signs of a drop in demand.

The Power of the Right Mentor

This prompted me to go and seek some information from the experts. At the time I did not know it but I was looking for a mentor. I had never even considered needing one, thinking that was only for sports stars and the like.

But the signs of fatigue were starting to show, and I knew I needed help. I found some much-needed advice from a high-profile mentor in the States.

His words are still ringing in my ears to this day, "**get out now while you still can**", because you guys Down-under will also be hit with the same tsunami we are about to be devastated by.

It's not that I did not believe him. No, I trusted he knew what he was talking about and had my best interest at heart. I just could not see how all of what was happening could unwind as quick as he said it would.

It did though, and just like the collapse of a multi-storey building, with us going down floor by floor.

The tap just turned off and as quick as it had started, it began to stop.

I likened it to the last puddle of water left in the height of the dry season on the African plains. All manner of animals including crocodiles, lions, tigers and an array of other unsavoury beasts, all fighting for the last scraps of water. Not a pretty sight – and coming down to the strongest surviving the drought.

The thought of losing everything I had been working for the last 20 years was overwhelming. My complacency and blindness to the important decisions – not spending enough time with my family, not investing my money wisely, spending too much on nice things – was now plainly evident.

The thing is, the cracks were appearing long before the start of the collapse, I just did not take the time to look at them. More, I chose to ignore them – I was bulletproof and the Ultimate Businessman after all.

I was on top of the mountain one moment and now all of a sudden I was toppling down to the dark valley below.

The holes in the bucket I could not plug quick enough, as I was haemorrhaging money and assets way faster than I could replace them.

So, how good do you think the quality of my thoughts were during this time? Do you think there were clearly focused on success and all of that I wanted to achieve in life?

Nope, my mind was a mess with thoughts of failure, embarrassment, not being able to provide for my family and so on, in a looping cycle, day and night.

Race car drivers are told to look around the corner, as they are travelling at such speed the corner comes up fast, so to look where you want to go makes sense. I was watching the wall at the end of the straight, travelling at 200 kms per hour and could not even see the corner.

Did I hit the wall and smash into a million pieces? Keep reading as everyone loves to see the crash even if they think they don't. I can tell you it does get a bit ugly.

CHAPTER 3

THE BUSY FOOL

CHAPTER 3

THE BUSY FOOL

I feel the need to warn you of the Busy Fool.

As if you're traveling full speed all of the time with your head down, anticipating changes in the terrain ahead will be difficult. More than likely you will not even see the wall at the end of the straight until it is too late.

I would often try and control every outcome, literally, running from one part of the business to the other trying to force a desired result. I think it gave me a sense of achievement that I was actually moving forward, this was an Illusion though.

If I could just stop for five minutes and assess the situation, look around at what was really happening, and listen, I would have gotten a good grasp of how stupid I was being.

The fear of loss and scarcity was driving me forward like an out of control freight train with no one at the wheel.

Have you ever been in a traffic jam on the freeway and watched someone franticly changing lanes, with a scowling look of anger and frustration on their face? Accelerating and slamming on the brakes continually, often nearly hitting the car in front as the build-up of traffic would, without warning, come to an urgent halt.

Meanwhile you have stayed in the same lane and actually gotten further ahead without any extra effort and not having steam coming out of your ears.

Trying to paddle against the current will be most often futile. I think maybe at times I was the smartest stupid guy in the room. Instead of going with the current and using it to my advantage, I would look for a strategy to build stronger muscles and fuel my body with the best foods so I could paddle harder and beat the current.

I would often get really annoyed at my staff and people in general who did not share my work ethic and also tried to do the impossible. I would think of them as weak-minded, lazy and more often than not would let them know how I felt.

Don't get me wrong **Strong work ethic is essential**, I still have no time for lazy people, but what is worse than being lazy and wasting your time?

Burning yourself and others out trying to paddle in the wrong direction.

How do I make the time?

I often wondered why some people seemed to have more time than me. It looked like they were just gliding along effortlessly and making a fortune in the process.

I would drive past a cafe on my way to a meeting and wonder how the people had time to sit around and take in the sights, enjoying the conversation.

How was this possible, and how are they able to free up time and make money so easily?

Friends of mine would always seem to be celebrating the next holiday to some exotic location, flying business class and staying at an exclusive resort with the private masseuse and all of the trimmings. I would often wonder, what's their secret?

Meanwhile, for me the alarm goes off, feet on the floor, sitting on the side of the bed and contemplating going back and hiding under the sheets as the scary thought of another relentless day would overcome me in a flood of emotion. Feeling stuck, helpless and overwhelmed.

But, just like I have always done, one foot in front of another, and get on with my day, rushing out the door, still chewing breakfast, a quick peck on the cheek of my wife, no chance of seeing the kids, as they're still curled up in bed, fast asleep.

Telling myself that one day things will be different, you just have to get through this next bit, and it will all get better, and I believed it to be true.

Feeling anxious about the day ahead, getting in my car and driving to the business with a churning stomach and tightness in my chest, thinking about all of the To-Dos, problems to solve, bills to pay, staff to deal with and that's just up until 9am. Is there a better way?

I was always at work first because the owner should be there first, right? I needed make sure I set a good example in front of the staff, running around and getting everything ready and set up for the team, so I could pave the way for them to have a good day.

Thinking of myself as the fix-it person, all day fixing problems. The more I fixed, the more arrived, one after the other in a never-ending procession.

Maybe it would be easier if I had a fire engine parked out front with a steady stream of water putting out all of the fires, but no matter how much water I put on the flare-ups, the moment I had one under control the next has shown up to challenge me in a new and unique way.

Telling myself to stay active because "you know you're strong you can handle it right?" "When the going gets tough, the tough get going", and all that stuff.

The early mornings, the late nights, taking work home after work. I found myself working on the weekends.

My social life started to suffer as I could not seem to stay awake, falling asleep at the restaurant table. Aware too of the concerned looks and comments from my friends and family expecting some level of engagement and attention, although I wanted to give lots of it, I could only settle for the basics, as more would take up valuable time in thinking, and on working on how to keep my head above water and make payroll for another week.

Meanwhile, everyone is saying I needed a rest – and not to work so hard all the time? Telling me I need some time off.

How would I cope with time off?! I would have to pull an all-nighter to get everything done in time – rush to document all of those procedures I knew needed to be done earlier, for someone else to try and manage all of my tasks on top of theirs. Coming to the rough conclusion that I would have to bring my laptop away with me once again to try and catch up between valuable time with my family.

The thought of so many issues to deal with before leaving – it would be easier to cancel the vacation all together. Not to mention all the things that could be going wrong while I was away, and the mountain of work I would need to come back to. It felt entirely overwhelming.

Again, I told myself that one day things would be different I just have to get through this next bit.

I really want you to think about this as before you know it, days can roll into weeks and weeks into years, as you may find yourself in a repetitive cycle stuck in the busyness of business. Mechanically going through life, running from one thing to the next, touching everything but not spending the valuable time necessary to create something truly meaningful for your life.

Just when I thought I had things under control and there may be some light at the end of the tunnel, a curve ball from out of the blue blindsides me and smacks clean in the side of my head.

What is going on here? Why do these things keep happening? I'm a good person, I have not wronged anyone. Why me?

The truth is I had asked for it – as I was the business owner I had the opportunity to create everything around me – good, bad or otherwise.

Just being a good person does not earn you the right to have an outstanding business. It would be easy to think and believe things worked in this manner, if it did I and many other good people of the world who give back to community, and service and help others would all be rich.

Money is just another form of Energy

The fact is only chaos comes to chaos, money and abundance seem to stay away, far away, not too different to trying to push two magnets together on the same poles. The moment they are forced together they are immediately repelled.

It is strange to think we totally get this, that magnets of the same poles are forced apart. It is an invisible force; you don't disbelieve it, as you can see it's a violent reaction to one another. The magnet demonstration is conclusive and true, even if it is not fully understood by most of us why the reaction is happening.

What was also not fully understood, or thought about, was the invisible effects from the energy I was putting out, frantically going about my daily busy routine, this would have a knock-on effect compounding over time and affecting people's view and judgment of me and my business. I can assure you the outcome was not a desired one.

Stress and its projection of bad energy are contagious, and like a virus often passed on to your staff, and at times your family. This is like a catch-22 – you can't win, as the busier you get to trying to catch up and overcome all of the problems, the less compelled your staff are to helping you solve the problem. So you find yourself with a bigger and bigger To-Do list.

How do you think your clients are going to feel about service delivered by disgruntled staff? My guess is that they won't put up with it for a moment, and more than likely will move on to a path of least resistance and choose to deal with a better business.

Loyalty does not carry the same strength that it did five, ten or twenty years ago, as now savvy people will only give you half a chance to get it right.

Be warned as **The Busy Fool** can creep up on you and take hold before you know it. Once the claws are in and injecting the poison, you may become blind to the effects as you view the craziness as the new standard. Unwinding from this situation is tricky, time-consuming, often painful and sometimes catastrophic.

We are all swapping value for money – if there is not enough value provided there eventually will not be sufficient money received. Without enough money will invariably come a lack of value, and so the cycle continues with 'lack' being the only outcome.

The reasons for not enough money or value are widespread and when caught in the grip of this downward spiral recovery can be challenging.

Often it is here where mistakes are encountered, as I was not spending the valuable time to assess the important matters in my business, too busy with the firehose, putting out all of the flare ups. As I was,

- Too busy to look at my profit and loss carefully

- Too busy to create quality systems, too busy to look at my customer service

- Too busy to build quality relationships with my staff and clients

- Too busy to notice I was going out of business.

Everyone has a breaking point. And I had reached mine, worn down to complete exhaustion, and unable to keep up the relentless routine any longer.

Only here, at this time, is where change can finally take place.

It always amazes why I, and for that matter most people, won't decide to change unless they are at the brink or rock bottom. So when it is the right time it's the right time, only you can decide.

We have all seen business owners looking much older than their respective chronological age – faces are like rings in a tree demonstrating the years – and their relationships are often severely damaged or destroyed. The bigger, costlier problems are often in the areas of wear and tear you can't see.

The vital organs are punished, the chemicals caused by stress can damage the heart and other organs leaving them vulnerable, plus the chemicals often pumped into ourselves to medicate the pain. Fast food, too much alcohol, cigarettes and so on all can leave their lasting effect.

This running style is not sustainable and, it is here I have witnessed business owners walk away, shutting the doors, being bankrupted, becoming severely ill, or seeking a cure for all of the craziness and getting help.

I'm always an advocate of the Get Help option, as there is always someone out there who has your best interest at heart and will have the skill, and experience to guide you through the transition out of The Busy Fool.

Some of you reading this Book will have been through a significant shift due to a change either initiated by you, the market, or simply life doing it for you.

If you are going well or just starting out in business, learn from the people who have done the hard yards before you. Get Help Before You Need it, as you never want to buy the umbrella on a rainy day.

The Past does not equal the Future

Not surprisingly, this was a very confusing process for me as a business owner, coming to the realisation that what I had been doing for so many years was now not going to work anymore, even though it did so well in the past.

I remembered a time back to my football career, I could kick the ball a long way but my accuracy was a little hit and miss. My coach recommended for me to change my style very slightly, as a result of the change, not only could I not kick straight but I had no distance either.

I wanted to go back to the old style as it was what I knew, besides I had a reasonable degree of success with it.

My coach was relentless in getting me to practice the new style, this frustrated me to no end as it was weeks until I was seeing any small benefits at all.

Slowly but surely, with disciplined practice my kicking improved to the point where I could shoot the ball off my foot like a gun and, with a large degree of accuracy, hit the intended target.

I needed to reach out and get help and find the adjustments needed in my business.

Most of the time we don't reach out for help as men and some women facing difficult times in business will often be entirely driven by their egos.

Hanging on so tight, not wanting to seem vulnerable, weak, or a failure. They tend to make poor judgment calls, based on what other people think about their circumstances – a strangely common behaviour, something I see all too often as the ego is brought alive by the fears we have. The fear of failure, feeling of a lack of competency, our identity being challenged and stretched at the seams.

These are all big stakes, and unless you have been through this type of challenging situation, it is very hard to walk in the person's shoes, as it can be downright terrifying, choosing to surrender to your fears and find the best way to move forward whatever that may look like. It is not until you're ready to open up to new possibilities and different ways of doing things, that you can start moving forward.

I knew I could not revert back to the Busy Fool I understood it would not work anymore, and the thought of it was much too painful, I could not go back. But what did forward look like? How could I do it differently and get the whole thing to work.

As most of the time we already know what to do within reason, I certainly had a lot of skills and knowledge. The difference in having the right mentor is they make sure you do what you know you need to do and hold you accountable for doing it.

I signed up for a recommended event in Sydney hoping to find the latest and greatest success formula to skyrocket my business.

Four days later I was on my way home and instead of having the secret source, all I had was lots of questions, a bigger To-Do list and feeling more overwhelmed than ever.

Everything was not lost though as a chance meeting on a five-hour plane flight from Sydney to Perth, set in motion a friendship that is still strong to this day and would change my perception forever.

I'm still trying to work out if she is an angel sent from God. I was certainly asking the Big Man upstairs for assistance but what I received was not what I expected.

Or maybe it was, as I asked for the secret formula I just did not recognise the packaging it came in as I had not seen it before.

No, glitz and glimmer, no bravado or ego, more softly spoken and with a confident unassuming smile.

A conversation that lasted the duration of the flight enabled me to tell her my story and how I was stuck in the Busy Fool and could not find a way out.

She said the words "I'll help you Glen", a welcome relief as the conversation was like no other I had experienced before. I knew I needed more, I just was not sure why, it just felt right.

There was no talk on the latest sales strategies or promise of a blueprint with the critical pieces left out required to put it all together until I handed over cash.

This was different, her unwavering help and support came directly from the heart, I could feel it.

Saying to me softly, "Glen you need to fix yourself first before we work on your business".

I felt like my kicking style was about to be changed again, instead this was about me needing to make adjustments to myself and then my business.

Getting out of your way.

Stuck in the firing line it is difficult to see the wood from the trees I needed to get out of my own way and leave the chaotic environment for at least two days.

A change of environment was the best thing for my bad case of Busy Fool, this was not about trying to work from home.

She said, "Glen you need to get out of your environment completely, and find a place to connect with yourself – a special place where you feel most comfortable and creative".

I love nature locations especially in the forest or sitting on the beach listening to the waves roll in, seeing the beautiful sights and views of the wonderful creations.

Where is it for you? As It is here and only in the fullness of the time that the hangover from being the Busy Fool starts to wear off. The filter slides down, and you can start to feel alive again and think about what's important and necessary for your life, family, and business.

For me I was feeling a little nervous, reckless and even terrified at the thought, "How can I leave right now while everything is such a complete mess?" And, "Who and how is the business going to run without me?"

It was a must to find a way to spend the time, this was not something small or insignificant, this was about my life.

I did not realise it at the time but science has proven up this phenomenon.

Trying to find ways to use more of our brains may be a myth as research has shown that shutting or slowing parts of the brain down and using less can open up channels and opportunity for increased ability.

Have you ever had the feeling or sensation where time felt like it stood still, or five hours when by as if it were fifteen minutes? Your sense of ego and self-doubt gets shut down or softened to result in a boosted state of confidence and creativity.

My time away had revealed insights, ideas, and significant shifts in my thoughts. I really could take a helicopter view of my life, seeing it all so differently, feeling a strong sense of clarity on what were the next missions I needed to complete.

Aligning with your mission

So how could you use this time for yourself to realign with your mission? Could you be guided by a sense of clarity and confidence you would not get in the busyness of business? Could this ensure the next steps you make are in harmony with what you are put here to do.

I know this may sound like a bit of hyperbole, but try listening to your inner self, as it is your inbuilt compass and one of life's secret shortcuts. This one secret could save you a lifetime of frantic running around aimlessly, and help you stay on your real course. Because your course is not someone else's expectations of what you should be doing.

No one sets out to do a bad job or have no inspiration in life, it kind of just happens, as we are herded, corralled, controlled and told to conform, and do what's necessary to get by, fit in and keep everyone happy. But we all have a higher purpose, a reason for being here and if you have not found it yet keep searching, never give up and listen, as I'm sure you'll feel it deep within.

It sounds counterintuitive, but the best way to help tease out your purpose is to let go and surrender to the process, to calm down the chaos and direct your thoughts and energy to bridge the gap.

Spend time in the now, don't worry about the past and stay out of the future so much, as imagining that there is no past or future to worry about allows you to just enjoy the now.

In the next chapter, you are going to learn about the one thing that is responsible for more suffering and hardship for business owners than anything else, and how you first need to Win This War of the Mind if you have any chance of succeeding at all.

CHAPTER 4

WINNING THE WAR OF THE MIND

CHAPTER 4

WINNING THE WAR OF THE MIND

Before you can *Take Your Business to the Next Level* or turn around a failing business, you need to win the war in your mind first.

I spent the time away from my business to get clarity but the moment I got back it was war.

Do you talk to yourself? Do you hear that voice inside your head? What is it saying to you? Is it commending you when you do a good job, saying "Well done", "You can do this" or "Congratulations, I'm proud of you"?

Or is it negative, saying, "You idiot, what did you do that for", "Stop being so clumsy and making mistakes" or "You're not going to be able to do it"?

Often what's going on inside your head is much more damaging than the reality of your current situation.

How is it that some people seem to be able to deal with adversity better than others? We have all heard the heart-warming stories of individuals who have been through catastrophic life-altering events and come out the other side as champions. While others will throw in the towel, the moment things don't quite go their way.

What is the contrast showing us that may reveal the secret pathway through the war going on inside our minds?

Intellectually, I understood that I needed to be positive, get clarity in my thinking and get clear on my outcomes. After all, that's what got me on top in the first place.

Only my mind was racing from one thing to the next; I was struggling to focus enough attention on the important tasks, instead being pulled in all directions.

What could you change about your thoughts to make a big difference?

> ➤ What do you think about all day?
>
> ➤ What percentage of your thoughts are negative?
>
> ➤ What percentage of your thoughts are positive?
>
> ➤ How could you calm your mind down to get clear?
>
> ➤ Are you focusing the solution or the problem?

I Had Lost the Touch

My magic wand appeared to be broken, as no matter what I seemed to do I could not reignite the engines of the business.

The work was drying up, and, as the business was geared up for volume, now that the volume had significantly diminished I had to plug the holes quickly.

I have always been strong and dominant in sales and marketing, so I drew my swords and tried to sell my way out of trouble. This definitely helped.

One part of me wanted to believe that things were going to come back and that the same strategies I had used to build the business originally would be enough to kick start the revenue again. But deep down I knew this was not the case, and that it was going to require something far more involved than doing the basics well.

No, I was going to have to overhaul the business and transform it if I had any chance of survival.

So why is it that most of us only instigate change when we are at the brink?

The truth is I was afraid of change, because I knew it meant getting my hands dirty and throwing myself back into the ring, knowing I would get my nose bloodied. My style of running the business had left me tired and run down, even in the good times. Willpower eventually runs out. It's not unlike the fuel tank of your car, and even though I had a long-range tank, mine was on empty.

So the thought of having the fight of my life to deal with scared the daylights out of me. I was resisting the inevitable. Intuitively I knew to avoid hitting the wall I was going to have to give it everything I had.

I was at a point of cognitive dissonance – two conflicting thoughts looping inside my brain with no possibility of an answer. I knew I had to put in a monumental effort, but I was tired, worn out and resisting having to commit to such a massive overhaul.

When your brain holds two or more contradictory beliefs or ideas it kind of short circuits. Human beings need an internal belief so that they can have consistency. It is a survival mechanism we all have.

At the time I had no consistency. I was hanging on tight, and I did not want to let go of the past, but the future was chasing me, mirroring my every move and ready to deal up my fate.

Our good clients were asking us to drop our prices, and even though they loved us they would have to go somewhere else if we could not oblige. I was resisting, as lowering your prices is a shortcut to going out of business fast, as I well knew.

Unfortunately, our competitors were dropping their prices to try and increase their market share; they were buying the business. It was getting ridiculous, and the pressure was on.

What could you change in your business to thrive in challenging conditions?

> ➤ What do you need to do to survive in a cut-throat market?
>
> ➤ How do you maintain your energy when you're always at full steam?
>
> ➤ Does your business need a serious overhaul?
>
> ➤ How do you maintain clients without dropping your prices?

Anticipating Change

There are not many guarantees in life, but one of them is that things will eventually change, especially in our modern world.

The speed of change in business happens at a lightning pace. Technology in our modern environment, designed to help leverage our potential, can often catch us unaware. It speeds everything up, solutions and problems at the same time.

Just when you think things are too good to be true, more than likely they are. It is at this time when everything is going well, and business appears to be moving in the right direction that you need to be on high alert. Certainly not kicking back with the cruise control on, resisting change or being complacent, as it will give you a false sense of security. The lag period from overindulging in the good times may just be enough to trip you up and undo all of your hard work.

There are many things I would have done differently with my time over to inoculate myself against the rising tide overtaking me.

Such as embracing the understanding that change is inevitable and will happen, almost like the seasons – it is a natural cycle. Often people will pull out the victim card when presented with change, or challenging situations, blaming their circumstances and what's happening to them, and not what themselves have done to cause the problem and what they should do to fix it.

Recognising you are a powerful creator, and results are your responsibility, you must own them. Having an action plan to anticipate change is highly recommended for any business.

Although it was too late for us to go back in time and create an action plan, we needed to change and start asking better quality questions.

So what questions do you need to ask in your business Right Now?

> ➤ What do I need to change in my business Right Now?
>
> ➤ What was working and I needed to do more of?
>
> ➤ What was not working and I needed to do less of?
>
> ➤ What does my business need to look like to survive the future?
>
> ➤ Who could I leverage off to help me and the business?

The problem was I had primed myself for a fight, and my mind and body were listening, over-riding my rational brain with high emotions.

Fear

Why was I so confused and clouded in my judgment?

My head ached with a dull, painful feeling as the night seemed to go on forever in a looping cycle of uncertainty and anxiety. Tossing and turning over thoughts of the unfortunate things that could happen tomorrow the next day or in the future.

As business owners, we can face these terrors often, and when you do, there is no mistaking them.

I think all entrepreneurs have experienced this horror at one time or another; it is inherent in our DNA. The very powers we possess to create and build empires can also work against us and quickly turning years of hard work into Big Trouble, and at times complete destruction.

Like a dark shadow following your every move just waiting for the opportunity to jump into action. Fear. Its sole intended purpose is to take control and dominate your decisions, actions, and ultimately your outcomes.

"Decisions based on fear in today's world are almost always not going to serve you well."

Most of us are unconsciously unaware of the affects fear has on our decision-making. What may surprise you is just how many decisions per day you make that may be dramatically influenced and affected by fear.

> " I learned that courage was not the absence of fear, but the triumph over it. The brave man is not he who does not feel afraid, but he who conquers that fear. "
>
> NELSON MANDELA

It would have been easier to throw in the towel and just give up.

I could not do that though; my core values will not allow it, I would think to myself over and over again. What about my employees who rely on me? What about our clients? What about my reputation? What about my family?

I was not big on sharing my thoughts with anyone; I would feel I did not want to burden others with my problems – I figured they would have enough of their own.

I was watching the money in my bank account disappear as I continued funding the business to keep it afloat.

I did not want to let any of my employees go. I felt sorry for them, plus I still wanted to have the capacity to deliver excellent service. I talked with my wife and shared my thoughts, and she said something very profound to me that day.

"Honey it was never about the money. Go out there and do you best, whatever happens, we will back you. You won't be happy unless you give it your best shot and neither would I so do what you need to do."

What an incredible boost of energy this was for me.

I think the first thing I needed to acknowledge is that I did not need to do it on my own and to stop being the lone runner taking on the world. This one thing made the biggest difference and is responsible for the achievements in my personal and business career that I'm most proud of.

The power of having the right mentor, supportive partner and family can often be overlooked. They have the amazing ability to provide the right tools, love and energy to you when it's needed most. Right in the middle of an emotional roller-coaster.

My wife was a real trooper when it came to helping me through the toughest times of my life. I am forever grateful for her unwavering love and support.

What strategies could you use to support yourself during challenging times?

➤ How do I stop waking up at 2am in a pool of sweat?

➤ Have you ever thought of throwing in the towel?

➤ Are your profits diminishing consistently?

➤ What fears do you need to face to move forward?

➤ Do you have someone to support you through tough times?

Fight or Flight

Our brains appear to be in need a 'software upgrade' – the programming of our ancient brains fight or flight response still alive and well today. Although far more suited to a much earlier time, we are hardwired, armed, ready for action, like a built in safety mechanism protecting us from the win–lose environment our ancestors called their home.

"Not a nice place to live" – never more than one wrong decision away from becoming another creature's lunch. Not hard to see and understand how important this unique system was in earlier times.

Some of us have learned to control this, or may seem to have a lower sensitivity to feelings and actions. However, we are all hardwired to meet basic needs for self-preservation and comfort.

In cave man times, it would be life-threatening to be indecisive about threats to our survival. These primal dangers we respond to are caused by a stimulation of a part of your brain known as the amygdala. Stimulation of the amygdala causes a variety of intense emotions, such as aggression or fear.

These areas of the brain control automatic responses, because without thinking too long they initiate immediate action. This more primitive part of our brain communicates with the rest of our brain and our body to create signals that are overwhelming and cause us to take urgent action.

Thus, the 'Fight or Flight Response' – a physiological response triggered from situations deemed to be dangerous or fearful.

We are meant to feel fear – it is a normal human emotion in response to danger or an imminent threat. The cocktail of drugs flooding through our bodies enables us to react promptly with appropriate action. Running away, fighting, or staying completely still in a frozen-like state to avoid being spotted by a potential threat.

In our modern concrete jungles, there are no tigers waiting to pounce, interestingly enough, but still this response, designed to protect us, is triggered in our modern world all too frequently.

Now for most of us, our daily life does not consist of fighting or escaping predators anymore. The trigger in modern day is much more sophisticated and widespread summoned from our internal chemical lab in everyday situations.

The outcome of these feelings, encountered on a daily basis, eventually causes intense symptoms, designed primarily to enhance the way we function so that, like a rapid-response team, we can jump straight into action with a heightened sense of awareness.

Our heart rate goes up, arteries and blood vessels dilate, breathing increases taking in more vital oxygen, adrenal glands go into overdrive, releasing adrenalin to initiate the response. Extra energy is created through the release of glycogen from the liver, as well as decreased activity in the intestines and slowing of digestion, all designed to keep power where it is needed most.

These dramatic changes in the body's physiology can bring on an increase in anxiety and, as the triggers are constant, anxiety can persist, giving us the feeling something is wrong.

This looping can create a 'fear of the fear', setting off unwanted experiences and feelings of anxiousness, we latch on to questions like, *how am I going to pay my bills?, what will people think if I fail?* – the list can go on and on.

Fear is often spoken about as **'false evidence appearing real'**. If you can catch yourself thinking and acting out on the possibility of a not-so-favourable outcome, you can start to break the cycle.

Remind yourself that there is no evidence yet that this will happen or has happened, as realistically the future is not the now, so dying a thousand deaths in the meantime will probably not serve you well.

> ## Focus on where you want to go, not on what you fear."
>
> ANTHONY ROBBINS

What are your motivating factors causing you to react badly?

➤ Are you focusing on your fears too much?

➤ Do you react to situations too quickly without thinking?

➤ Are your fears real or something you have conjured up?

➤ Do you feel like life is one big fight to stay alive?

Fear and Your Mind

When a fearful situation is presented, your amygdala is highly aroused, triggering off the production of chemical responses, and making connections within the brain which cause us to behave in a certain way. It is thought that some people have more sensitivity to fear, due to increased activity from the amygdala and associated connections in these situations.

Regardless of what we tell ourselves, there is a contrast going on in the mind, doing the exact opposite to what we want to happen. Up front, you are saying I've got this! You know what you are doing! You have practised this before etc., only for our subconscious to put the brakes on, as it is our subconscious that is controlling our every move.

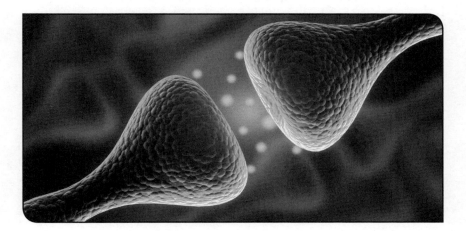

If you have any doubts of the control your unconscious mind has over your every action, just think about what keeps your heart beating 24 hours a day, and what keeps you breathing while you are asleep. (We will go deeper into the power of your subconscious in later chapters.)

Quite simply, feeding your mind with thoughts of fear will have a detrimental effect on you reaching your goals, just as feeding your mind with knowledge and ideas of success will have a positive effect.

 Inaction breeds doubt and fear. Action breeds confidence and courage. If you want to conquer fear, do not sit home and think about it. Go out and get busy.

DALE CARNEGIE

The Effects of Fear on the Body

> 66
>
> You can feed yourself with the best quality foods on earth, if, however, they are washed down with bad thoughts and fear, the results can be very unfavourable.
>
> 99
>
> GLEN MICHAELIDES

Our finely tuned bodies are made to handle stress. Think of the body like a race car. Talking it up to the Red Line is not a problem, however leaving at full RPM all the time... well more than likely you will blow your engine up. Not a good idea for cars, and certainly not a good idea for our bodies.

The modern environment can make it difficult to stay stress-free and, unfortunately, most people fall in line with the chaotic, fast paced hyper-world most of us now call normal. The body then responds to the stimuli by releasing hormones, the main one being cortisol, produced in the adrenal cortex. It's a typical response to stress.

This hormone plays some vital roles in the human body – it helps us deal with stressful situations. For instance, shutting down functions which is deems unnecessary at the time, like the immune system, to direct our energies towards dealing with the stressful situation at hand.

This 'burst' if you will of cortisol and adrenalin is meant to be only temporally – just long enough to get you through the stressful situation. However, in today's modern world stress can become chronic and this is where it becomes a problem.

You may know of people who are constantly stressed and always getting sick? Or how a person in this mode will often get sick just as their holiday starts. We usually put this down to bad luck, but is it luck or is it a body too overwhelmed to cope anymore?

Pain, heart disease, digestive problems, sleep problems. Memory issues, an inability to concentrate on tasks, poor judgment around decisions. All are possible symptoms of chronic stress.

Something to think about. As you will appreciate, it can be very hard to take yourself to the Next Level while caught in the grip of fear. Spending the time to identify this silent killer and stamp it out is a must.

Freedom from fear

Would it be possible to get through challenging situations if I just let go and stopped worrying about what might happen? And concentrated on bridging the gap?

What could you do to help combat overwhelming fears?

> ➤ If today was your last day would all of the petty things matter?

> ➤ Always do your best to make a difference with everyday action, it will keep you moving in the right direction.

> ➤ Understand it will get messy and chaotic before the situation can improve.

> ➤ Stop worrying so much about the future and failing, instead concentrate on being the best you can in the now.

> ➤ You will fail – try and make the failure smaller, but remember often failure is an intelligent, normal way of getting better.

> ➤ Study people who have mastered adversity and overcome impossible situations to become World Class.

> ➤ Hone your skills and knowledge – this helps you with choices and gives certainty to move in the direction of success.

> ➤ Have a clear outcome and goals for your life. Fixate on the idea of yourself having already achieved your goals.

> ➤ Run towards your deepest fears and meet them head on as facing up to what scares you most is the best way to dissolve the power it has over you – you are the only one giving it the power in the first place.

I'm not suggesting it's as easy as 'click your fingers, and all your problems will disappear'. No, it is sheer hard work and will take guts and determination for you to have even a remote chance of making it.

For me, I finally made the decision I was going to give it everything I had and put all of my energy and efforts into getting back on top. Strangely I felt relief in the decision. I think that was because my mind was not so conflicted and I had started to set clear intentions in what I wanted to achieve.

This gave me clarity and an extra boost of energy I did not think I had, what I learned from this was when you are at your most tired and worn out is when you get to see what you are made of.

Continually showing up is 80% of the road to success, not giving up like 95% of people do in demanding times.

It got me thinking about anything of significance I have achieved in my life, how at first it was hard to get going and build momentum. The painful first week of the new diet; the gruelling exercise programs; the chasing my girlfriend and now wife of twenty-plus years around to get her attention; the challenge of training myself to get up at 4am and see the next project through to completion, no matter how cold, hot, wet, windy or rainy.

It's okay to feel like giving up. No one is perfect all of the time. But to push through, to stay on track in the midst of pain and hardship, and to not give in when everything and everyone is screaming at you to do so – that's the difference between making it out of the orbit, or struggling to get off the ground and staying in your current situation.

Only you can do the heavy lifting to build your muscles. There is no satisfaction or growth in others doing it for you. In business and, in life 'You Must Participate in Your Own Rescue'.

You might just find the muscles you are building are not strengthening your body – in the next chapter, you are going to learn how everything could just be "The opposite to what you think" and how to use this knowledge to your advantage. And inoculate yourself against what others are not seeing.

THE OPPOSITE TO WHAT YOU THINK

CHAPTER 5

THE OPPOSITE TO WHAT YOU THINK

We have become addicted to thinking that the game of life must be complicated to Win. And have succumbed to thinking it is an absolute impossibility to win in all areas.

But quite often the answer to the problems lie in their visible simplicity and not in some long-winded convoluted, complicated formula. More often than not when the simple formula for success is laid out in front of us, we don't see it, and even if you were to see it, we don't believe it can work.

Why is this? Why do we overcomplicate things to the point of sabotaging our success? Why do we procrastinate, confuse and paralyse our thoughts?

More often than not if something you are doing is not working it may require the exact opposite approach as getting the basics right seems to be a big problem. Why?

As mentioned in the previous chapter our natural instincts have a bias wiring us towards moving away from pain. Now this is an **Extremely Strong** desire its primitive original design and function was purely designed to keep us alive.

I was letting this strong, primitive wiring dominate my life, when problems appeared my default programing would take over my rational mind. Taking me off course and not acting in accordance to my true values.

Having the right mentor's soothing energy allowed me to see things I previously could not, as she did not have the same level of emotion attached to the problem as I did, so there was no interference, just a clear signal.

She could see what I was doing and said to me "If you had ten million dollars in the bank and money did not matter would you be doing things differently?".

I realised I was acting on instincts and not intelligence I needed to fight these strong urges deeply conditioned inside my brain if I was to have any chance of getting it right.

Success Leaves Footprints

I started to notice that some people had mastered the overriding factors of the **Negative Bias**, I figured all I had to do was stop acting from a place of overactive emotions and just follow the clues.

If you want to be successful in any area of your life, study the people who have walked before you and are a living breathing example of what you are trying to achieve.

If you want to learn how to drive a car for instance, you could take advice from someone who has read many books on the theory of how to drive a car.

But that is not going to be the same as someone who has been doing the actual driving and has mastered every scenario, problem and who overcame adversities along the way.

I needed to override my emotions of a threat that was urgent and very real, as there was a strong possibility of losing the last of everything I had worked so hard for.

Not an easy thing to do I can assure you, but it is an absolute must if you want to overcome the powerful effects of the Negative Bias.

I had stopped focusing on the most important things that had made me so successful in earlier years.

ROR – Return on Relationships, providing maximum value many times over before I even thought about asking what's in it for me? I used to be relentless at customer service for no other reason than I loved to help, and it was simply the right thing to do.

Have you ever been caught up in chasing the next quantum leap from false promises?

What about the next fancy complicated diet, including the new mysterious pills guaranteed to lose 5 kg overnight?

Let's not forget, the blueprint business formula secret that only the rich know about and you need to get right now before stocks run out.

Are we just lying to ourselves? The truth is that most of us are looking to hit a home run every time we swing the bat. Why?

We love the romance of the brilliant complex strategies used to overcome whatever the thing is we think we need to overcome. We don't want to be in the trenches day after day doing the basics, the one percenters that add up over time and make the real, sustainable differences.

Who wants to do the boring stuff? No, we want the exciting theatre of how, in spite of all odds, adversity was surmounted and the incredible riches achieved, by the secret amazing formula, found only in one remote location on earth at the top of an ancient mountain.

We pump ourselves up for the ego-fuelled conversation at the next breakfast meeting, on how our brilliant new sophisticated strategies will be used to crush our opposition.

What if it was not about the big stuff? As most of it is a built in distraction method designed to pull our attention away from dealing with the bigger problems and what really matters.

Doing the little things. Let me explain, what if it was about lots of little seemingly insignificant wins, culminating and adding up to creating valuable balance in all areas of our life.

If we look at sports and take for instance the game of basketball, the winners of the match are the team which scores the most points within the allotted time frame.

Two points from inside the arc and three points from outside, now yes you can win the game with a three-pointer and often games are won with a three-point shot on the siren.

However, if you have a look at where the majority of points are scored the largest percentage always falls into the repetitively trained textbook shots at the hoop. Not the fancy complex shots from half court.

So in this example, it is understandable to see how the essential 'in the trenches' scoring makes up the bulk of the winning formula.

Now this method is not unique to basketball, or any other sport for that matter, it applies throughout countless industries: business, personal growth, weight loss, fitness and the list goes on and on.

As all the power is in the small consistent, measurable improvements. So I apologise if that may seem boring and dull, as I would rather you have great sustainable foundations that can continually be improved upon.

The good news is that even though it may seem boring and not highly relevant, it is easy to do. As you're not learning how to be a brain surgeon, just keeping it simple and chipping away one piece at a time.

Instead of cutting down on product, find ways to add more value to your offering.

Instead of removing all bad foods from your diet start by adding more good foods.

Employees will tell you they are leaving for money reasons; the truth is more than likely they are unhappy with the little things.

Your family says it's ok when you're always working back late, but they are suffering from it and want nothing more than to see their mum or dad.

Instead of saying you are too busy to take the two weeks' vacation, take periodic long weekends.

Instead of trying to get things perfect start with small measurable changes and build up to the full version. Otherwise, your frantic rush to quantum leap will leave you feeling desperate, overwhelmed and ineffective.

As, more often than not, it is the exact opposite of what you think that is required to enable circumstances to fall in place. Meaning if you want things to start working, 'you need to show up in a different way' and think differently from where you are currently at.

I have a restaurant that I like to go to, and have been eating there for the last three years. I love seafood, and they do the best grilled platter, cook it just the way I like it, and the chef always comes out to say hello. It's the little things I'm attracted to. Like the free dinner voucher on my birthday, and the one free drink with my meal.

One night, turning up at the restaurant and ordering my usual I found the plate to have noticeably less on it than normal. It was overcooked and lacked some of the trimmings I had become accustomed to.

Putting it down to them having a bad night I let it go a little frustrated, understanding that every business has these small indiscretions.

On returning the following week and ordering the same dish and finding, the same substandard quality, and quantity as the previous week, I had to ask the question. It seemed out of character for the owner to let this happen in his restaurant.

Interestingly the restaurant, unbeknown to me, was under new management, and when I quizzed them about the difference in quality and quantity of my favourite dish I was told that was normal and how we do it now.

You probably have guessed how this ends, let's just say you don't get too many chances to get things right in business in today's economy.

Instead of the restaurant cutting corners and costs to try and save money, in a mad panic to make their investment back, the exact opposite formula would have been the right option.

Counter intuitively we need to find new ways to increase the value and continue to stack it up, so the client never has a need, want, nor opportunity to leave ever.

So let's have a look at what the restaurant has missed out on with my LTV **Life Time Value.**

Approximately 60 meals a year including my wife's at an average cost of $110.00 for both including some drinks.

60x 110= $6600.00 x three years = $19800.00

Now if we look at the referrals we have recommended who not necessarily eat as often as we did at the restaurant 15 people over three years $23500.00

Now if we also take into account the family get together and Christmas party's another $4800.00

So we are looking at an LTV at $48100.00 over the three years. Now if you take into account that if the food and poor service continued to be substandard what would the next three years look like?

A loss of $48100.00 this from only one good client as you can see this situation is and will continue to be massively detrimental to the business.

Now let's consider all of the other high-quality, long-term clients who may also decide to leave for not putting up with mediocre product and service.

How long would it take to the restaurant which was doing a roaring consistent trade would be in real trouble? My guess is not long, also considering if the new owners woke up to their poor choices and tried to turn things around how long would that take? What would be the cost?

So that is one example that could be plausible, right? But if you feel you need a little more convincing of the Life Time Value of a client then read on.

The primary costs are in acquiring new customers, the marketing and offers to get them in the door, the nurturing along and all the effort and time in building high-quality essential relationships.

The problem is once we have the new client we immediately go looking for the next new customer and forget about our new most important person in the world.

My staff would often say hey boss, how can I help? And I would immediately correct them and say in a loving way, let's get something straight I am not your boss, I am not the boss, the clients are our boss as they are the ones paying yours and my wages. So given that fact, they are the number one for any business.

Let's have a look at the second demonstration. I love my health and fitness I have trained and studied all over the world, but will often be a member of the same gym for ten years at a time.

Now I have just left a gym after ten years of paying my membership month after month year after year for all of those ten years. Why did I leave? Well interesting question, the gym started to deteriorate. The equipment became worn out, and the popular machines were always in a state of decay.

The cleaning was not regular and as a result, people would often get sick due to poor hygiene of the equipment and bathrooms.

The regular email updates and communication on special offers and tips and tricks had stopped.

No, thank you letter and free offer for ten years of membership, no upgrades vouchers, in fact, no correspondence at all.

Looking back over the ten years for me going to that gym was more a matter of convenience, as it was five minutes from my home and business.

Then a new gym was built and opened only ten minutes from my home, in a convenient direction. Moreover, they took the time to send me an offer explaining all of the features, benefits, and cool free stuff to get on board.

I figured it was worth a look, Wow – new state-of-the-art equipment, an in-house masseuse, juice bar, clothing, apparel, supplement packages, free training towel, free sessions with a personal trainer. Not to mention lots of clean showers and passionate, caring staff.

As you could imagine it was a no-brainer. I left the gym of ten years and joined the new one.

So let's look at my LTV Life Time Value of 10 years, $55.00 per month for ten years, $6600.00, Drinks, weight belt wrist straps over the years $300.00

Referrals, ten people, three of whom have also stayed for ten years – $29800.00

So the LTV for me to the gym was $6600.00 + $300.00 + $29800.00 = $36700.00.

As you can see the figures don't lie and the effects of losing a client are much deeper and widespread than most take the time to realise. Even if you halved the figures, it would still be a significant loss.

The crazy thing about all of this is that they did not even call to try and talk me out of it or incentivise me to stay. I just walked out after ten years of patronage never to be seen again.

The Paradigm shift: a different way of looking at your business and yourself.

Let's face if we are honest with ourselves, we are in business to make money and why not make a lot of it as you have gone to a lot of trouble to get things set up to this point?

The one problem is many try and make money without thinking about the demonstrable benefit for the client. What is their motive for action?

They are not turning up to help you with early retirement, meet your ever-increasing costs or fund your next holiday.

It is well and truly on your mind, but not theirs, in fact, all that is generally on the potential customer's mind is "what is in it for me?". That's it – they don't care about you, or your bills, or your next holiday, nor should they.

What's more, your clients and staff for that matter have a built-in polygraph detector that goes off the moment you try and put yourself first and forget about their needs and wants.

This hurry to be financially free brings up a strong competitive frequency, pushing away the very thing you are chasing so voraciously.

On the other hand, by relaxing and calming down the energy you are putting out, you can enjoy the journey. Look for the balance along the way even though this may seem counterintuitive.

Would you rather be financially free in five years with worry, stress, problems, being overwhelmed, sickness, pressure, and sadness all day every day, or would you rather take a few years longer to be financially free, and enjoy the journey along the way?

Which path seems like the smoother, easier and a more enjoyable option to you?

I know what you're thinking: "I don't want to have to wait one second longer than I have to achieve my goals and become financially free." I get it.

I am not suggesting for a moment that you cannot quantum leap your business, however, if you study most of this fast improvement, overnight successes stories, nearly always you will find it done on the creative plane and not the frantic competitive one.

How much extra time would you have if you were not stuck in the Negative Bias? Wasting time thinking about all the things that could go wrong.

Ego

As it is often said, you need a big ego to reach, succeed and survive at the top of your profession. So what is our ego? That is the part of you that wants to make it on your own, and show the world that you are special and that you can do it unassisted. It's the force that causes you to judge others in colour creed, religion, looks, beliefs – the list goes on.

It is the voice in your head that says "get out of my way I'm coming through and if I want something done I'll do it myself" because no one is better than you, right?

However, it is our ego that keeps us in this state of being overwhelmed and in fear as its primary job is to look for fear around every corner.

Yes, we need our ego – it has a purpose of keeping us from making fools of ourselves, however when it goes into overdrive and is given too much energy and attention, that's when the trouble starts.

Because it is in ego-fuelled, blinded states that poor decisions are often made, resulting in either holding you or your business back or propelling you to do something detrimental and often very foolish.

We all have an ego, the main thing is to be more conscious of it and work on keeping it in its place, under control and not the forefront of your actions.

So what would your business and ultimately your life look like without interference from your ego? Your higher purpose will, manoeuvre to the forefront and take control as this is the part you were born to play.

This allows you to assert your natural harmonious connection to the universe, allowing a more effortlessness flow. When you get into the habit of not letting fear, guilt, pressure or anxiety control your daily thoughts and emotions, your actions will be represented in a smooth more effortless quality, allowing a different type of energy to work with you, instead of against you.

Whatever your mission in life find people on a similar journey or who can help guide you through don't try and do it by yourself. Yes, you have to do your heavy lifting, but not work everything out on your own.

You will be surprised how amazingly events start working in your favour as there is a supporting, caring essence in the universe that wants you to be abundant and prosperous. Its sole purpose is to support you in your creations from thoughts and actions.

So what is the secret to aligning with this incredible universal power? Practise staying out of your ego and in the creative plane.

Practise being happy and grateful for what you have Right Now as there is always someone a lot worse off than you and your current situation.

A trip down to the Children's Hospital ward is usually enough to get over your insignificant problems and back on track.

> The formula for success.
>
> - Get clear on why you want what you want.
>
> - Be certain of the reasons.
>
> - Feel confident you're on purpose.
>
> - Take massive action toward obtaining your worthy ideal.
>
> - Beliefs=Actions=Results=Beliefs

If you get off track and find yourself caught up in the clutter, go back through the above steps, as what you are clear on today may not be as clear to you in time.

Don't be slow to recalibrate if you drift off course, as you are going to make mistakes and run into challenges many times over and over – it is meant to be this way as it forces us to grow.

So just breathe deeply and let go, have faith rather than hanging on so tight and trying to control everyone and every event. As you can't fit any more knowledge in your hands and heart if your ego has the largest grip on your reality. Take your ego out of the day-to-day and know that many have walked this path to find the biggest successes they ever imagined.

Just remember if you're enjoying the journey and you're on purpose, and you have put the steps into practice for the higher good, you will be successful. It is the law of the Universe as in this space comes, strong foundations to make the best quality decisions.

CHAPTER 6

THE DECISION

CHAPTER 6

THE DECISION

Now I had made the discovery that the road to success was the opposite to my previous thoughts and actions. I knew that deciding to save my business was a must and that I had a very big *why* for wanting to do it, I could now start the process of rebuilding.

So was this the right or wrong decision? How do we know if we need to let go and cut our losses? Or fight on and give it everything we have?

I didn't know at the time, but I had made a decision to rebuild right or wrong and was sticking with it until the end.

I made the decision to sell my house and most of my larger assets, the ski boat, cars, toys, and I pooled all of my money. I can tell you this was not an easy decision and attracted a lot of attention from family, friends and the like. I think mainly they we worried for us but displayed it in the strangest ways, always putting their foot in their mouth with unhelpful comments.

Seeing what was happening with us and the decisions we were making, I think scared them. It made them think of the possibility that they could also lose what they had worked a lifetime for. As if it could happen to us anything was possible.

It was heart-wrenching having the conversation with my wife that we would have to sell the family home. We had just got it perfect and felt like we could happily live there a lifetime.

You know something though? As hard as this was I always had her unwavering support, knowing that no matter how bad things got we had each other. And I was supremely confident I could make it all back again and do it bigger and better next time.

I knew it was not going to be easy, I had to make the best quality decisions.

So when have you ever made a decision that was a must to achieve? Did it turn out to be the right or wrong one? Do you wonder to yourself *why did I make that decision?*

Are you a smart person, that has made stupid decisions making no sense whatsoever?

I'm happy to put my hand up here, as I would often make decisions in my business that, intellectually, I knew were wrong, but I still made them anyway. Why? Well until I understood what was driving my decisions I could not create a model for correcting them.

Did you think to yourself why do I keep doing this, I know it is not serving me but, as if on autopilot I seem to make the same mistakes time and time again?

The thought flashes into your head or the words just come out as if spoken by another person not you; it's almost like your standing on the sidelines like a spectator listening to yourself speaking someone else's words and not your own.

Now, some of you may be aware and conscious of what I'm talking about, for others now I have brought it to the forefront, pay careful attention to your decisions.

Think to yourself what emotions you are feeling at the time of making the decision. Fear, frustration, love, excitement, selflessness, curiosity, luck – what are your dominant states of mind you go into before making decisions.

This will go a long way to helping you understand your decision-making process and why some of your decisions have been empowering and well serving, and others have had dire consequences on your quality of life and wellbeing.

> **It is in your moments of decision that your destiny is shaped.** 99
>
> TONY ROBBINS

➤ What state are you generally in when making decisions?

➤ Are you influenced by other people too often?

➤ Have you put off a making a decision for fear of facing it?

➤ Are you on autopilot when making decisions?

➤ What is the dominant question you keep asking yourself?

Let's dig a little deeper as to what's going on behind our decisions and driving us to make them. It seems we all have our unique way of looking at the world. The information that comes in is filtered through our unique lenses.

The filtering process is shaped by our upbringing, beliefs, and events that have happened in our life. It's almost like we have our internal compass guiding us along our path. Some say this internal guiding force is also passed on through our genes.

Most importantly it is the meaning we place on the events of our life that dominate our thoughts, feelings and actions.

Have you ever wounded why someone would want to be a firefighter or a police officer and **Significantly** put themselves in harm's way even if they knew coming out alive of certain situations would be in doubt? How can some people make it their life's mission to help others and selflessly **Serve** when they have so little themselves?

Or, has it made your toes curl up to think of the **Variety** of jumping out of a perfectly good airplane and skydiving, or bungee jumping off a ten-storey bridge with a rope tied around your legs, hurtling towards the rocky river bed below?

Do you know individuals who are **Certainly** too afraid to leave the house, or try something new and go outside their comfort zone? Preferring always to stick to the status quo, in complete contrast to people who are always willing to **Grow** and better themselves, and who purposely get into uncomfortable situations and try new things.

We all have a dominant bias towards one or more of these controlling forces – created, conditioned and reinforced throughout our lifetime.

If you think about it carefully, you will discover your dominant bias. Look back on a previous decision or decisions made. What were the forces at work in guiding you to make that decision? And how has it shaped your life?

Take note of people you know or come in contact with. What controlling forces are working in the background, guiding their decision making? Learning what is influencing other's decisions is imperative in helping guide you and others to better quality outcomes.

Have you ever thought about an important decision and what would have happened if you had made it differently, how your life could be dramatically altered and on a future path right now? Now, if you can remember back to what was influencing you at the time of the decision, you may get an *aha* moment as to why you went in that particular direction.

Was it because you were afraid to change out of your current situation, so you stayed put for fear of failure? Did you decide that things were a little annoying, so you needed to fix something that was not broken? Or that you decided to do something because you were told it could not be done, compelling you to take a larger risk than normal and losing out big time?

What about helping friends or family by giving them large amounts of money or loaning your car to find they were in no hurry to help in return?

As a result of your decisions are you finding you keep making the same mistakes time and time again? Based on autopilot decision making?

Decisions are often carried out without thinking them through or without a deeper understanding of how you should think them through and why. We tend to get ourselves in all manner of situations saying yes to requests that are unachievable or not in line with our nature. Usually these decisions come to bite us on the back end.

Expectations are often not met causing conflict and stress through over-promising and under-delivering on a decision, not in line with your values or morals.

Many people will often say no to spending time with the family or loved ones, because of being too busy with work and other urgent and important projects.

The real regrets come from deciding not to put family first and spending quality time with them – putting on hold the family vacation or dream trip as they were too tied up in the busyness of business and other time-consuming activities.

Procrastination and the inability to make a decision on important matters could be holding you back big time when it comes to moving forward in business and life. Putting your head in the sand and not making a decision, right or wrong, will put you in a state of being overwhelmed, confusion and frustration.

As with critical decision-making, most of us will be highly motivated to move away from pain. It is a hardwired defence mechanism, built in to protect us.

A motivation of moving away from a current point – let's say A – and moving toward B would be that A is a more dangerous or painful place to stay than B. And if B is perceived as a more pleasurable place, the move will be easier to make.

Many other driving factors than fear may initiate decisions that lead you to move from A to B. People will change their situation because they are too bored, or they do not feel they are growing anymore, or that they are not being given the recognition they needed to receive for their efforts. Money will also come up as the factor, however, it is not normally the primary contributor in the decision, more of a catalyst. The fact is beliefs and filters are unique to each person, and we all have a dominant setting that drives our own.

When staying at A and moving towards B are *both* considered dangerous and/or painful this is the making of procrastination, as you cannot decide the safer option, given that the evidence suggests similar pain staying or going – causing you to stay stuck.

But rarely it is the case that evidence is suggesting equal danger either way. If you delve deeper and look at what is driving our perception you will invariably find your filtering system to be hard at work in hiding the truth.

To take another example, that nagging cavity is not actioned for fear of the dentist's drill, for instance. However, deep down, you know the somewhat tolerable cavity could turn into something much more severe. You finally summon up enough courage to visit the dentist to find it was not that bad and that in contrast, the pain you were putting yourself through in a state of procrastination was far worse than the time in the chair.

Finally, procrastination can be more than just putting your head in the sand – interestingly it may have to do with our left- and right-hand side of our brains.

The left-hand side of the brain is more dominant in language, processing what you hear and taking most of the speaking duties. It is also responsible for logic and mathematical calculations.

The right is more creative centred – able to comprehend visual imagery and piece together what we see. Imagination, intuition, and insight are strong features along with holistic thought and music awareness.

If our brains are imbalanced through exhaustion (maybe too much time on the computer and a myriad of other possibilities) rebalancing your left- and right-hand side may help to give better clarity in making decisions.

Getting leverage

You decide whether you are happy or sad, you choose if you are the Victim or Victor.

 The Brave Don't Run, face your fear look it in the eyes, take a deep breath and do it anyway.

GLEN MICHAELIDES

I needed to get leverage in my business. I wanted to grab it by the scruff of the neck and drag it kicking and screaming into submission and profit. But I did not have the energy for that and besides, that is no way to run or rebuild a problem business.

I needed to bring on more clients **or so I thought** and enlisted the help of a good friend of mine to add to my knowledge of sales and marketing. Having someone in your corner seeing the things you cannot can be the difference between success and failure. They can take an unemotional view of what is really going, on seeing the 'out of the jar' experience you may be missing.

But a word of caution here before you enlist the help of anyone with your business. Always ensure they have **Five Times** more knowledge than you about the chosen subject and, most importantly, have your **Best Interests** at heart. There are countless people out there waiting to pounce on tired, worn-out business owners, in the grip of fear and overwhelm looking to make a quick buck.

And don't be scared to ask for a list of their achievements, as you may be taking advice from someone who has less knowledge than you do and is only reading from the manual.

Now over many years of helping people with their business and lifestyle success, there is one thing I know to be true.

It is all about having the right mindset and taking control of your emotions. This is the best blueprint strategy, custom-designed for success. Anything else will have almost no positive effect, especially if you are making the wrong decisions based on overwhelming fear and a flawed model for making decisions.

I myself had attended countless seminars, read books listened to CDs, etc., and absorbed a lot of information over the years – however, until I got a real understanding of what was driving me from behind the curtain I could not leverage the information correctly and make lasting change.

Obsolete Decision Making.

You see, our values, beliefs and the way we filter information has a huge influence on our decision-making process, in fact, it is the main driving force for our every action.

Remember, understanding what is behind our decision-making processes and that of others is the key to making the change.

So, we need to identify if our standard way of assessing and making decisions is flawed, due to our (flawed) perception of the truth. Did we just automatically respond in line with our biases or opinions. Are we using an **obsolete** built-in protection system? One that, with your new-found knowledge, you can identify and reassess, with a different set of eyes?

And could this new way of looking at your decisions save you time money and anguish in circumventing poor decisions? And will it allow you to also help others in identifying the woods from the trees.

My understanding of the processes controlling me and, therefore, my business was fundamental for me to have any chance of recovering. I would go on to use this knowledge to its fullest extent.

So, how do we identify these beliefs and filters to get movement from A to B – assuming going from A to B is what is required? To answer that question, we need to look at the meanings attached to the events that can form beliefs.

Meanings

Understanding the meanings, we have attached to our past, and will attach to current and future events will open up a 'behind the curtain' view.

Starting right back to a time of our first memories, meanings placed on events can and have shaped our lives, then and now. Resulting in our current situation and determining where we will be in our future.

In fact, due to the unique way our brains absorb information from birth until around seven years old, seemingly unimportant events could have been, back then, life altering in empowering and disempowering ways.

Fears around failure, success, shyness, phobias, unrealistic expectations, guilt, abilities, and the list goes on and on, all possible results of meanings we place on experiences.

As we are only born with two fears – the fear of falling and loud noises, all other fears are learnt, so I believe they can be unlearnt.

Think back to a time when something did not go your way, it may have inexplicably failed even after you have made sure to put your best foot forward and the hard work in up front.

Did you give up? Did it get too hard to continue? Did you play out the victim card? Did you ask Why does this always happen to me?

Or did you think that the reason was that there is a much better opportunity coming your way?

I would often think that there was some force conspiring against me and my business, as, at the height of everything going wrong, you just could not make up the crazy stuff that appeared to be happening **to me** at the time. So many unexplainable events that I could dedicate a whole chapter to. I think you get the message though as I now know even as ridiculously insurmountable the situations faced the time, that was not truly the case.

I was actually being prepared with a vast array of experience, learning how to overcome almost unsolvable problems. Experience I now get to share with you and many others.

What if life was actually happening *for* you and not *to* you? And all of the events in our lives were an opportunity to grow and learn.

Do you think you would you have different meaning attached to events if you believed life was really all happening *for* you?

I can assure you, you would, as I am not just giving you a reading of the instruction manual, more real-life experience and the keys to an alternative future. Only you can decide the meanings to the events in your life.

Remember, it's not your past that makes you who you are today, more how you respond to it.

The Subconscious and Decisions

As I alluded to in Chapter 4, your subconscious (or unconscious mind as it can also be known) is what is doing all of the work in the background. When your conscious mind goes to sleep, your subconscious is wide awake and in fact, goes into overdrive. The subconscious mind is known to operate seven seconds ahead of the thinking conscious mind and is responsible for controlling 95% of your behaviour throughout the day.

Your subconscious mind:

- stores memories,

- organises memories,

- represses memories with unresolved emotions

- presents memories to your conscious mind and preserves the body.

We see, hear and feel our way through life, and throughout all of our experiences our brain logs each event. Some call it a timeline, an unlimited memory bank that permanently stores everything that has ever happened to you.

This data can be recalled to help keep us safe. For instance, as a young child when you touch a hot stove this information is logged in the brain as a reference point that can be recalled at a future time, sharply reminding you that the stove could be unsafe or hot.

This series of life events creates our unique pattern and beliefs, subconsciously ensuring that you respond correctly, the way you have been programmed.

Now, remember a time when you felt emotionally and physically uncomfortable. Was there real cause for concern/did you need to take action? Or perhaps was there imminent danger approaching? Or are these feelings brought up because you're trying new things and changing your regular pattern of behaviour, i.e. going against your standard programming?

You may feel pulled backward towards your comfort zone each time you try something new, be conscious if you feel tense or uneasy. Your thoughts, emotions, filters and meanings will all be hard at work running programing in the background.

Remember, top performers in any field who have decided to *Take Their Business to The Next Level* are always consciously aware of the growing pain, and are always pushing themselves out of their comfort zones and enlarging their circle of support, so it gets larger and larger with each new venture.

They know full well that staying in their safe zone or bubble may seem ok and comfortable for now, but it is an illusion, and will not last or achieve the Next Level in lifestyle and business.

Knowing this, it's not hard to imagine what effect behind the scenes programming could be having on your decision making. But even if you start small at getting out of your comfort zone, keep at it, as the muscle builds so will you expand your territory and along with it your level of success.

1. Identify and understand what drives you.

2. What are the meanings you have around the decision?

3. Take some time out to reflect before making a decision

4. Make a decision – don't sit on the fence, put your energy into it.

5. Feel confident in your decision as you reached it though intelligence.

6. Give your decision a completion date and stick to it.

7. Take massive action on your decision don't half do it.

8. See it through to the finish line – don't give up too early.

Through hypnosis, repetition to form new habits and energy modalities, will enable you to reprogram your subconscious mind for success. The conscious mind, empowered with positive thinking and creativity, will set in motion manifesting your wishes and desires.

Now that you have a platform for making good quality decisions let's look at getting some real traction on your decisions to greatly leverage your results. Giving you some serious speed and momentum necessary to transition from where you are to where you want to be.

CHAPTER 7

BRIDGING THE SUCCESS GAP

CHAPTER 7

BRIDGING THE SUCCESS GAP

One of the biggest challenges for people in life and business is how to Bridge the Gap, from the place you are currently at, to where it is you want to go. Most want to do this in the shortest amount of time and with the least amount of effort.

I can certainly attest to this. When you are in very uncomfortable situations in business you will, at times, want to do almost anything to get out of trouble.

So, after many years of testing these theories on myself and other business owners, I have had lots of success, failure and learned many lessons.

Looking back on the times I have failed to bridge the gap, I simply have not followed the plan – I've tried to shortcut baking the cake, only to have it flop and not turn out right.

Having learnt a new powerful model for decision making allowed me to be very conscious of the reasons behind the decisions I was making. This new model was making a profound difference not only to me but my business alike.

You might remember in previous chapters you read about the importance of getting crystal clear on your outcomes and vision. Knowing the target gives you a place to aim (note if you are not clear yet on what you want to achieve, go back and get crystal clear, as without clarity you will get an unclear result).

This is probably one of the biggest stumbling blocks for people in business and life. As It's like setting sail without a compass, or a rudder for that matter, and expecting to get somewhere remarkable.

As Bridging the Success Gap can often be about discovering how to bridge the gap internally first. I had learnt some valuable strategies and tools on how to build this internal strength and fortitude.

So I could now look externally to find someone who had mastered what I was trying to achieve. Not just anyone, but someone who has been highly successful in doing that very same thing so that I could model their success.

Too many people try and reinvent the wheel or build a better mousetrap, only for it to fail miserably. I'm not suggesting innovation is not a good thing – on the contrary. But figuring out what is the success formula and innovating or improving around that will more than likely increase your odds of success, and leverage your results.

There are countless coaches and mentors available to help you. Find someone who is extremely successful at what you want to master and, as important, has your best interests at heart.

You will find developing a relationship with these high-quality people will be very lucrative for you, as most will happily share their secrets and do their level best to help you achieve your desired outcomes. Importantly, they will shortcut your learning curve and help you become successful sooner.

Personally, after many years of doing it on my own the hard way, I realised the power of mentors and coaching. Roughly calculating I would have spent the equivalent of a new Ferrari, on personal development over the years. When I tell people that, some understand, and others would say "you are mad, I would rather have the Ferrari".

The point is, what would be the point of owning that type of car, as without the education and the skills required to be successful, affording this kind of vehicle would be doubtful in the long run?

Besides the right mentor could see 10x return on your investment. That being the case, you need to find a way to pay for the best.

As at the time of writing this book I have four mentors, all with different fields of expertise, from health and fitness, spiritual, energy, marketing, and understanding how our mind and body works. Speaking from experience the benefits are nothing short of amazing.

A good coach will stretch your thinking and get you to go for larger more challenging outcomes. They will provide the foresight, skills, strategy and encouragement necessary to make the gap easier to cross and your goals more likely to be achieved.

Whether you are a business owner, training for the Olympics, a top CEO for a Fortune 500 company, or The President of the United States.

If you want to be successful, hiring a coach in your chosen field is the secret weapon, as the best in the business aim to continually improve in their chosen field and stay at the top of their game. Improvement to your knowledge base should be a never-ending quest if you want to continue dramatically to bridge the gaps in your life and business.

Hard books, audio books, CDs, DVDs, seminars, podcasts, YouTube are just some of the media you can use to improve your knowledge base.

Habits of success, you will find the experts in bridging gaps have the best kind of practices, and they maintain and protect them religiously.

As everyone has 24 hours in a day, so why is it that some people are always saying "I would love to have the time to do that"? "That" could be reading a book, spending the time to exercise, taking the day off to go to a seminar, or improving their diet and preparing good quality food.

Now, there are lots of different statistics on this subject; however, it is said the average American watches more than four hours of TV a day – that's 28 hours a week or two months nonstop per year. Compared to Australians at 24.25 hours a week.

Even if you halved the statistics that's still around two hours a day spent watching the latest episodes of whatever's the hot topic at the time.

Couple that with our ever-increasing addiction to smartphones and computers and you have already taken a significant chunk of time out of your available day.

Everyday distractions such as phone calls, emails, unscheduled appointments and emergencies – guess what, you have eaten into a further significant chunk of your time.

General unnecessary chitchat with staff and colleges around the office will burn your time also.

Living your life reacting to situations and not planning your day is an excellent way to get yourself miles off track, burn up your time and sabotage your results.

Let's take a look at the success habits of the experts, as this will give you some workable solutions you can use to get some time back. Firstly, you will invariably find most will:

1. Wake up before the sun around 5am; this is a two-hour head start on the masses.

2. Exercise for at least 40 minutes to get their body tuned up for maximum performance.

3. Have a healthy breakfast and plenty of water.

4. Meditate.

5. Consume educational material.

Even if you added just these points to your strategy, it would make a profound difference in many areas of your life. As these important rituals are completed before the average person even wakes up, let's have a look at the rest of the day. So what else could you do?

6. Plan out the most important outcomes for the day and stick to them religiously.

7. Catch up on emails three times a day morning lunch afternoon, and turn it off in between.

8. Don't answer unknown phone calls.

9. Block your daily calendar out on the most important items that must be achieved that day and don't vary from the plan.

10. Don't let people hijack your time with their problems, unless they are life-threatening, book them in at an appropriate time and the problem will sort itself out.

11. Don't make excuses, continue with your progress and the plan.

New Ideas: It is said there are not many original ideas left, just countless new or different versions of an existing idea. I'm not sure if this is true or not, but if you think about it, we all had to learn from someone. Information has been passed down from generation to generation, business to business and so on and so on. Sounds plausible right?

This leaves some unanswered questions about how our ancient ancestors managed to build monuments like the Great Pyramids and Stonehenge, to name two of many examples of unexplained constructions all over the world, made with such accuracy and skill. How did they dream up such information, did it even come from this earth? Who did they learn the skills from? There are many possible answers to these regularly asked questions.

There is another theory and it is way out there, this theory suggests that we have all the information inside of us from birth. An untapped knowledge base that, we can draw on to solve any manner of problems and dream up fantastic ideas and innovation.

It is waiting for us; all we have to do is find a way to tap into the well and bring forth the wisdom we intuitively know. For me, I believe all of you have most of what you need already inside, some are not ready, and for others, it is bubbling at the surface and cannot wait to get out.

It is said "when the Student is ready the Teacher arrives" – when you are ready the right person will come along and tease this inbuilt information out by trusting you, encouraging you, listening to you and teaching you to bring it forward.

Life has an ingenious way of staying in equilibrium, a kind of universal law. If you take too much from one area, you will lose from another. If you give more than you receive, you will get more back. Trying to bridge the gap by force and at the expense of others losing, or not being true to your morals and values, will eventually result in the gap widening.

Letting go, and trusting in the process, I would often ask myself "What does that mean 'letting go'?".

I would grapple with that question many times, until one day I finally got it. Before I did, I could not understand the difference between letting go and giving up, and I was not one to give up or let go without a fight. It would constantly hurt my head to think about giving up and just hoping it will all work out, it sounded reckless to me and felt like I was sitting on my hands.

It reminded me of a quote from Confucius:

 Man who stand on hill with mouth open will wait long time for roast duck to drop in.

Metaphorically I did not want to go hungry, so I wanted to go out and chase the duck down, cook it and eat it.

Neither did I have the patience to wait around forever and hope for the best opportunity to show up on my doorstep.

To be clear, I'm not suggesting you wait around and hope for the best, but on the flip-side running around drawing your sword and trying to force the outcome all the time is not sustainable and you will eventually burn yourself and others around you out, from being overwhelmed and exhausted.

Bridging the Success Gap operates from a space somewhere in the middle of pushing too hard and just giving up. Think carefully about the following, don't leave any steps out in baking this cake as you don't want your business to be a flop.

1. **Get crystal clear on what it is you want to achieve (keep the end in mind). Ensure that there is a high want or need to support your achievement.**

2. **Fill you mind with high-quality information and thoughts, speak only a language of abundance.**

3. **Always come from a place of serving at a high level with the best interests of everyone involved, ensure every transaction is mutually beneficial to all parties.**

4. **Design and document the systems and strategies to support the Vision and Mission and set them up to run on autopilot.**

5. **Custom build your team to deliver on the promise, arm them with the necessary knowledge and skill, never stop training, nurturing and supporting them, always.**

6. **Innovate and create to claim more market share.**

7. **Perfect your product to make it a high-quality, high-value, sustainable, predictable offering.**

8. **Make building your database a priority as it is a currency for your business. Use a client relationship system to send the regular communication.**

9. **Market your creation and in so doing express your X-Factor, your point of difference, uniqueness. Understand the psychology of your target audience and tailor your message to suit.**

10. **Test measure and record data, and don't stop adjusting based on the facts and figures.**

11. **Get high-quality testimonials as this provides a dramatic demonstration of your prowess.**

12. **Treat your customers and clients like Gold.**

This may seem like a lot of work. However, I can assure it is worth being prepared to put this work in, as the consequences of not doing so could cost you a lot more time, stress and money than you ever imagined.

Step number twelve in baking your cake? Treat your customers and clients like gold as they are where the cash comes from to keep your business alive. May just be one of the most important steps to the recipe. The relationship with you key clients should be on the level of good friends and not clients. To simply know their wants needs and desires is not enough.

Take the time to really find out what they are all about, who their other family members are, when their birthday is, what their favourite foods are, etc.

Once you have established this type of relationship, there is a deep emotional connection between you, one not easily broken by your competitors, even if the pricing is much cheaper.

The following six steps are a tried and tested strategy that, if applied correctly, will make a significant difference to the strength, revenue and longevity in your business.

They are the blueprint revenue driver required for any business to be successful. Executed correctly you will see the results very quickly.

---

1. To Increase Leads

Optimise your lead generation so that you drive more high-quality leads for your business. The following are some examples of media you can use to do this.

- Social media: Facebook, YouTube, Instagram, Snapchat, Twitter

- Website

- Trade shows, open days

- Competitions

- VIP Clubs and loyalty rewards

- Webinars, Seminars and educational

- Affiliate partnerships

Now that we have more leads coming in through the various forms of media generation, step two is

2. Increase conversions, by adding massive value and take away objections up front, as if there is a particular reason they won't buy.

Converting the leads, rather than having a shortage of them, is often where business can fall over. Here is where you need to measure all of the data find out why you may not be converting at the highest level.

- Have a script: so the potential clients learn up front why you are worth dealing with. It is here where you need to tell the story.

- Follow up: this is a must, and if done correctly with significantly up your conversions.

- Strong guarantees: stop them in their tracks and create massive trust.

- VIP Clubs: offer benefits, extended warranties, priority.

- Finance packages: allow affordability now.

- Prizes and giveaways for quick action-takers.

- High quality quoting system with information brief and photos.

- Record conversations for training purposes.

- Take larger deposits that give a stronger commitment to the client following through.

- Free audits to identify weakness in the product they are currently using.

3. **Increase the number of transactions through follow-ups, incentives, regular contact, offers, promotions and educational material.**

- Have a client relationship management system to automate correspondence and nurture customers and clients.

- Regularly offer loyalty discounts.

- Provide high-quality information that will benefit your clients in line with their interests.

4. **Increase referrals – have a number of referral strategies set up ready to reward the referrer.**

- Give a gift for referring a friend.

- Provide a loyalty card.

- Affiliate commission structure

- Allow them to ascend in store value, the more referrals made.

5. Increasing profit means you charge accordingly for the huge amount you give; good quality clients will pay more for high-value products such as:

    •   Extended warranties.

    •   Added bonuses.

    •   Free inspections.

    •   Better quality products.

    •   Added additional services and products via your business.

6. Increase the lifetime value of your customer – the costs of losing a client as covered in previous chapters can be very expensive.

    •   Acknowledge them for their patronage.

    •   Give them a gift on their birthday.

    •   Offer them VIP service on their next visit.

    •   Make them feel special by giving them personal service.

Let's not forget the lifeblood of the business and why we are providing all of this value. I cannot stress this point strongly enough.

CASH FLOW – without it you have **NO** business, so these two words are the most important. Take the time to understand the meaning of them, never take your eyes off the flow of money in and out of your business.

Now, once you're satisfied that you have you action steps in place, you are fully operational and can Bridge the Success Gap. Congratulations, you can now trust in the process, and let go of worrying and stressing about everything else that could go wrong.

I'm not suggesting anything else could go wrong, but in business you have to be always prepared for the unexpected. I'm merely suggesting constant worry about what may go wrong after you have done your best to be your best is dangerous. If you are doing your best, you have made your intentions clear; you are on purpose, and you will in time be rewarded for your efforts.

This may all sound like I am giving you a harsh dose of reality – because I am, this is a tough sport we are playing. I need to make sure you are as fit as possible to create, thrive and operate at your best.

Now that you have strong foundations in place, concentrate on where you want to go, not so much on where you are now.

Focusing on the past, future and all of the reasons why you can't bridge the gap will leave you stuck in the now. Look more to the outcome you want to achieve, see it in your mind's eye, speak of it as if it was already there, act as you would act if you had achieved your outcomes already.

Feel the excitement in your body, do this often and believe it to be true, as it will be as true as you decide to make it.

Most people give up too early, they set themselves up nicely for success and then give up right before the benefits start flowing. Understand that there is a delay period between all of the efforts you are putting in and the result.

Usually, unknowingly, you're right on the brink of the breakthrough when things are at their toughest, you are doing everything right to the letter, but the ducks are just not lining up. DON'T GIVE IN as success is within your reach. Give an extra push and make some small adjustments if necessary, as it is here you will find your real genius.

Never forget about the importance of language in business. Life is full of contradictory statements that can sound very different to each other. Such as:

- Work hard/Don't be too busy.

- Create outstanding systems and procedures/Don't try and be perfect.

- Give high value/Don't be concerned to charge a high-end price.

- Be there to support your staff/Be ruthless on enforcing the consequences.

- Look at your current figures every day/Concentrate on the outcome.

> - Be disciplined/Be kind and supportive.
>
> - Beating your head against the wall and expecting your headache to stop is insanity/People often give up millimetres from the finish line and undo all of their hard work.

Finally, things were really starting to come together and I was seeing some Rubber to the Road improvement with my business this created some much needed excitement and energy.

Learning success does not lie in the potential you were born with, more how much of it you chose to capitalise on.

I had begun to Bridge the Success Gap and during the process discovered how to use newly found information that would quantum leap the strength and foundations of my business as a whole.

Fasten your seatbelt as in the next chapter I'm going to share some information that may change the way you see the movies of your mind forever.

CHAPTER 8

THE POWER FROM WITHIN

CHAPTER 8

THE POWER FROM WITHIN

Mystery, amazing intelligence, and riches beyond our wildest dreams, are not normally the language spoken by a down-to-earth person. Some things are not easily explained though.

I need to be clear here I'm not one of these people that is into hocus pocus. I'm pragmatic, logical, and I like to back up my experiences with scientific data.

However, there are some things that have happened during my life that I cannot fully explain, and I feel the need to share these experiences.

To leave them out would not give you the X-ray vision required to see the invisible, and to leverage from your power within.

I had started to lay down some strong foundations in Bridging the Success Gap by making adjustments to the critical checklist you learnt in the previous chapter, and was applying strong willpower and doing my best to master my thoughts.

Building from the success I learnt in bridging the gap, I started looking for clues, to how others before me had succeeded in spite of extreme challenging situations.

I wanted to take advantage of their wisdom and energy to find solutions.

I started looking at the ancient Egyptians, I figured if they could build strong foundations and pyramids consisting of as many as 2.3 million blocks weighing an average 2.5 tons. There may be some secrets I need to uncover.

How did they maintain the energy required to create such monuments, taking decades to build and using only primitive equipment in today's standards?

Did they have some extra help we are not aware of?

There are countless secrets and amazing facts these monuments and the people who lived in those times hold, more than I could fit in this book.

Something interesting that I discovered in my research was an Energy Source called the Wands of Horus.

These clasping cylinder-like objects are said to harmonise the two basic energy flows which the Egyptians called *ba* and *ka*, corresponding to yin and yang in the Oriental tradition.

They are said to regulate the energy balance in the body and have many health benefits, from the nervous system, cardiovascular system and insomnia, to stress – and the list goes on and on.

This includes eliminating negative thoughts and positively conditioning the mind to help manifest particular goals for the holder. This energy source is said to be amplified by the pyramid itself acting as a powerful cosmic antenna, strengthening the power.

I was looking for some super human energy, extra power to maintain momentum and continue to build on my success.

Thinking back, I had a hunch that we may already all possess this built in extra power on tap ready for action, but wondered how could I use it effectively in other areas of my life?

The Force Field

As an avid sportsman, I played football for many years and as a young man I learnt something that may sound strange, but that got me through the challenging times.

I was recruited up the ranks early. Although big in size for my age I was somewhat intimidated by the older players who had played professionally for many years. I played in a position where it was very physical and you could get injured badly as the game was quite rough in those days.

My coach could see that I was a little tentative about going in hard for the ball.

He pulled me aside and said "I'm going to give you a secret weapon". He told me that if I was concerned about getting injured when going in strongly for the ball than more than likely I would be.

He went on to explain that we all have an invisible force field that we can summon on request, that would protect me even in the heaviest of impacts.

He told me to remember other times in my life or when I had pure focus for the ball pushed through the pack and felt strong and unstoppable. He taught me to have an unwavering faith and belief that I could summon the force field at will. By bringing into my body the strong feelings of confidence, strength and success I had felt at times in the past.

Spinning these strong feelings faster and faster until my body was tingling with energy, excitement and confidence engaging the force field. The other part to this secret was the ability to see yourself already having achieved the result before the event actually happened.

I know this may sound strange to some, but it worked. I would see myself already kicking the goal, or seeing myself taking the mark before the ball was kicked towards me.

I successfully kept this advantage to myself throughout the rest of my career maintaining a reputation as a hard ball player with an ability to anticipate the play and outcomes to my advantage.

Now as I mentioned I am a pragmatic person, I need to know why, always asking questions, in order to get the real answers behind unique events.

Have you ever had one of those days where you were trying to get out of the house, and every time you tried to leave you realised you have forgotten something and have to go back inside.

Backward and forward – no matter how hard you try you cannot seem to get it together, then finally you make it to the car to find you have left your keys inside.

I was having one of those mornings but instead of slowing down I started to run frantically as I was going to be late, finally I pulled it together got in my car and on the way.

The windows on my car were misted up due to an unusual cold winter snap we were experiencing at the time. I could see out of the windscreen but the side windows were all fogged up.

Only minutes away from the office I entered one of the last intersections something truly strange came over me I had a lifelike premonition I was in a car accident. I felt the impact and after that it was like I was in a washing machine getting thrown around forwards, backwards and sideways all at the same time.

Intuitively I engaged my force field, this event seemed to go on for about seven seconds, as quick as it started everything went back too normal.

Not so – instantly, I felt an extreme violent impact to my driver's door I did not even see it coming as my window was still fogged up.

A large vehicle had gone through a stop sign and ploughed into me travelling at some serious speed, with enough force to rip the engine completely out of my car.

I was tossed all over the place like a rag doll and when the chaos come to a stop my body was in a state of shock, all I could see was smoke quickly filling the vehicle, I could strongly smell fuel that was pouring out of a large rip in the tank and as I looked over I could see the car that hit me had rolled over on its side and was pushed up agenised my passenger doors.

I needed to get out, but the impact was so violent that none of the doors would open. I summoned all of my strength and kicked out the back window managed to pull myself out and collapse on to the floor.

Thankfully a passer-by had come over to help drag me away from the precarious situation, as by this stage the vehicle was on fire. I must have lost some time as I remember coming to sitting down on the curb at the side of the road.

It was almost like my hearing had sound control and the volume had just been turned up too full. As I could suddenly hear the sounds of the ambulance, and fire brigade sirens in the distance.

I was struggling to focus; I didn't realise it but blood had been dripping down from my head and over my eyes.

I looked up trying to focus through my blood-soaked view to the calming voice of a paramedic asking me softly what my name was. I had to actually think about it before I could answer. I finally said my name and added "but I'm ok and I don't need to go in the ambulance".

To that she replied, "Well I think you actually do you have a nasty cut to your head". I put my hand up to my head to find I could feel my skull as I had split the side of my head open and sustained a serious concussion that would require many stitches and literally hours to put back together.

Understanding the Instruction manual

Neuroscientists are suggesting that the conscious mind is operating at 100 miles per hour and in contrast the unconscious is working at 100000 miles per hour.

Current research equates this to our subconscious minds operating a full seven seconds in advance of our consciousness.

Was I experiencing this phenomenon in the form of a premonition allowing me time to engage my force field, and potentially saving my life? As strange as it sounds I really do think that is what happened.

Scientists, with a large degree of accuracy, can predict a subject's thoughts when asking them to choose a number between one and ten, by actually knowing what they are going to say in advance by looking at their brain patterns with specialised equipment.

It is said almost like we are carrying a halo of predictability around with us – we are here and now, but it would be possible to predict our actions seven seconds before we are even aware of them.

Meaning you have more than likely made you mind up about something seven seconds before you were consciously aware of it.

Think of our **conscious** mind as the pilot in control of the flight simulator, the pilot is in control and everything is going well he moves the controls and the simulator reacts perfectly.

Now I want you to think of the unique programing the flight simulator is operating under as your **unconscious** mind.

No matter how well the pilot is flying the simulator, the program has built-in challenges like taking out one engine, or a hydraulic failure. Regardless how much the pilot feels he is in control, he may not be able to counteract the program and the simulator may crash or take some serious damage trying to land. Or maybe not even take of in the first place.

We all have a built-in flight simulator in our brains as we get to test drive experiences before they actually happen.

If I was to say I have baked a delicious cheesecake that I want you to try it, you can use your simulator to think about and see yourself eating and experiencing a rich creamy delicious cheesecake.

What if I was to say that I filled it with fish guts instead of cream? Have you just taken your simulator for a run? Did you imagine the taste would be terrible? Would this pre-flight simulation stop you from eating the cake altogether?

So what programming are you running in your subconscious mind, or flight simulator that you may not be aware of holding you back Big Time.

Have you put up artificial barriers up in your mind creating roadblocks, not unlike border check points slowing you down because of limiting thoughts, controlling your permission to move forward?

Things had started to make sense and I was putting the pieces together, as thinking back to anything I have ever achieved of significance or in contrast the areas of my life that did not go according to plan, were all a result of my programming.

It was all to do with the Power within – if used positively I would produce the desired results. Like seeing my wife in my mind before I had even met her, buying my first house, becoming a business owner, having two children, the list goes on.

Think back to your life's achievements, or not-so-desired results, as understanding anything we want to achieve firstly requires us to see it in our minds.

If I asked you to think about sitting in a roller-coaster and experiencing the sensations of the ride, you would first need to make a mental picture, almost like watching your own internal cinema screen. The movies we see are different for all of us, however have some unique similarities.

There may be some of practise required for you to recognise and become aware of your images and your internal voice. (And no, your internal voice does not mean you're crazy, – to the contrary.) Ask yourself where is my internal voice? So did you hear it? It is slightly different for all of us, keep a mental note of where yours is.

For me I reached the conclusion that my outcomes had more to do with me, and the pictures I was creating in my mind, with the size, sounds, and volume level also dramatically influencing the effect of my results.

The Power Within requires a different way of using your brain one that will take some practise. I can assure you it will be worth it though, as I and many others are living proof of the amazing benefits you can achieve through this process.

Understand things can go wrong, please know the past doesn't equal the future and letting previous problems continue to run your life is not going to serve you well.

*Often it is not the actual event we are so traumatised by, it is more to do with the intensified meanings we place on experiences in our past. Our meanings are not things that **we have** but things that **we do**.*

What if we could change the meanings placed on events so they do not feel the same anymore?

How many opportunities have you missed out on due to your interpretation of the events in your past? As the perceived intensity of the event is often distorted, blown out of proportion, or even invented out of thin air in our minds.

What if our minds had the ability to control our outcomes and heal the body based on how we think? Sounds impossible? I can tell you it works, and there is a lot of research proving it *is* possible.

The power of suggestion and placebo effects are well documented – from people who have died from a missed diagnosed illness they never had, to spontaneous remission from patients told by mistake they were healthy and sent home from hospital with a potentially terminal illness.

There are also well documented facts with amazing results from patients given placebo sugar tablets, which performed equally well as prescription medicine. Studies have also shown the brainwaves of placebo users, after being told they were given a wonder drug, to be significantly different from people not taking anything. The Power from within is stronger than you may think.

Stacking your experiences

I want to give you some tools to leverage from your own ability to get amazing results. Earlier in this chapter you read about the force field and how it protected me in challenging situations.

Given the fact business owners are often bombarded with challenges from all directions, the force field can come in handy.

As it can also make you feel Outstanding, strong, intelligent, confident and resourceful anytime you want even for no reason at all. We are going to engage a strong force field, so even if you think this is silly I want you to do it anyway, because if you don't do it, it will not work.

Think back to a time where you felt fantastic, I mean Really Fantastic, you might already know the one I'm talking about, it may even bring on a cheeky grin. If it doesn't, it's not what you're looking for. Find a better experience.

What did you feel at that time, I want you to see it in your mind as if you have just stepped back into the very same experience that you have remembered?

Excited, with butterflies in your stomach – it makes you feel so good just thinking about it, as you can even sense a smile coming on just behind your lips.

The more you think about it the better it feels and the better it feels the more you enjoy the sensation. Pay careful attention to where this feeling starts in your midsection, I want you to be conscious of this energy travelling upward to the top of your head.

Right before it leaves your body in your mind's eye, I want you to grab it and bring it back into your body, let the energy travel back upwards and again grab it and start it spinning form your midsection to your head and then back again in a circular motion.

Get it going faster and faster until it is spinning at a fast rate of speed, the faster it spins the stronger the emotion and the stronger the emotion the better you feel. Keep it spinning faster and faster until your body is tingling with excitement, happiness, confidence, intelligence, strength.

Feel this energy inside you and know we are designed to work with these unseen forces, as our brains are actually prewired and ready, so don't be surprised just how good you can actually feel. Keep practicing as you will get better and better at feeling great for no reason at all.

Whatever the beneficial emotion you want to experience, go back to a time where you felt that resourceful state, recreate the experience you had at the time, and simply repeat this simple energy exercise with as much intensity as you can.

Listen to me very carefully –do this once and it will make you feel better, do it weekly and you will feel great, do it every day or even five times a day and you will be amazed at the results.

You will literally hardwire this process into your brain, setting up your subconscious, and reprograming your flight simulator with a dream program, so it responds in amazing ways. Remember **If you don't do it, it will not work**.

Now that you know how to practise feeling fantastic any time you want, let's look at getting rid of the unwanted movies playing in your head, so you keep the lessons but lose the negative emotional meanings.

Think of it as creating chemicals of mastery (not misery) in your brain.

You would not leave dirty handprints on your new sunglasses, so why would you want to leave them in your mind where you can see them every day?

Moving Forward

Ok I want you to think about an experience that you don't want to feel bad about anymore.

Now close your eyes and point into space where you see the unwanted image from your past.

Have you done that? Ok, now I want you to close your eyes again and think of something amazing that you want to have happen in the future, again pointing in the direction to where you see the compelling image.

Draw an imaginary line between the two and you have just identified your timeline. This is important as it will help you with the following exercise.

Ok let's go back to eliminating your unwanted experience – when you see it in your mind is it large like a cinema screen? Is it in colour? Do you feel the experience? or maybe hear the sounds from the event?

As bad, unwanted experiences will often be in full life-size with all of the trimmings. See this life like movie on the cinema screen in your mind, spend some time to focus on the vision – do you have it? Ok, now I want you to immediately white the image out to a pure white screen. Now if the image comes back immediately white it out again.

Keep doing this until the image is pure white, now I want you to push it off into the distance to the direction you originally identified its origin came from.

Picture the colour draining out so it is now faded dull grey, now shrink it down to a quarter of its original size and continue to push it further away until you can only just make out the vision of the experience.

Now make it even smaller to the size of a pea then smaller again to the size of a grain of sand and then see it simply picked up by the wind and blown away into the distance and out of sight altogether.

Then, again see the vision, white it out, drain out the colour, push it away, shrink it down till you can hardly see the image, then make it smaller and smaller until it floats away in the distance like dust.

Keep doing this until you don't feel the same way about the problem anymore. You can do it as many times as you need to feel strong and empowered.

Feeling Fantastic

Now I want you to think forward to a time in the future where you have created exactly what you what for your life. See it on your cinema screen, but this time instead of shrinking it down and pushing it away I want you to expand it out and bring it up close so it looks larger than life. See it in full colour, hear the sounds and feel how good your new future will be. If the old image comes back I want you to snap the new image back into its place, bring it to the front and make it full size. Keep doing this as many times as you need to and as often as you want.

How do you feel? No doubt fantastic. Is the intensity of the unwanted experience only a portion of what it was before? What about the experience of your new future, is that bright and exciting?

Ok you may choose to repeat this exercise as many times as you feel necessary, depending on the intensity of the meaning you have placed on the event.

The good news is it takes no time at all to do and it really works, so now you have some powerful tools you can use them whenever and on whatever you feel you need to. Feeling fantastic on cue or knocking out unwanted limiting beliefs.

So you can now activate the power within and are ready to use your skills to get some much needed Rubber to the Road.

CHAPTER 9

GETTING RUBBER
TO THE ROAD

CHAPTER 9

GETTING RUBBER TO THE ROAD

'Starting with the Right Vehicle' is imperative now that you have learnt to harness the power within, stepping up the momentum to create your Ultimate Business in the form of a V8 performance vehicle and not an old bomb, will give you the power to move forward faster with less effort.

All too often I'm working with business owners who transition directly from their job or hobby straight into business. Mechanics will often start a mechanical workshop. Personal trainers may decide to start a gymnasium. Plumbers and electricians will often start businesses in their respective fields. Likewise, a chef might open a restaurant. And I'm sure you understand the list goes on and on over all types of demographics.

We don't often receive the 'Running of the Business' skills required to grow and prosper while we are in a job or hobby, and without the business, financial, systems, team, and marketing education required to successfully run and grow life can often be an uphill battle.

More often than not, most business owners have just brought themselves an expensive, time-consuming and stressful job.

Now, hands up who got into business to:

- Have less time

- Have less money

- Have higher stress levels

- Work longer hours

- Not see your family

- Have less fun

- End up with poor health?

This is a cold hard dose of reality for countless business owners all over the world; I have seen and witnessed it with my own eyes.

According to many conventional sources, eight out ten entrepreneurs who start a business will fail within 18 months – that's 80% who will crash and burn. Out of that only 4% will make it to over the ten-year mark.

It is too easy to ignore 'becoming a master at the basics', citing more complex reasons for problems and blaming outside influences.

Do you have a business or a job?

How do you know if you have a job, not a business? And are you a business owner, or a business operator?

If your company is not meeting your dreams needs and desires, you may be just that, having created a job description only you can fill.

The following five points are a critical checklist to see if you have a business or job, and nine key factors that will determine if you are heading for potential disaster.

1. Do you have the ability to turn leads on and off in your business?

2. Are you able to fulfil the inquiries on time every time?

3. Can you leave at will to spend time with loved ones and capture special moments?

4. Are you are making a good profit, not just a wage?

5. Do you have everything in place ready to sell it tomorrow?

Much research has been done on why business fail and the reasons can be widespread. The following have been factors I have witnessed:

1. Failure to crunch the numbers, so ran out of cash, did not hit the sweet spot.

2. Lack of marketing skills, for obtaining enough high-quality leads.

3. Lack of systems and accountability, for doing the basics well.

4. Lack of need for the product or service, no one wants what you are selling.

5. The wrong team, and/or a lack of training, delivering poor service.

6. Not building outstanding relationships with staff and clients.

7. Doing the right thing at the wrong time.

8. Trying to do it all on your own and not getting a mentor-coach to help.

9. Superior competition – they are just doing it better.

Responsibility

It is here that we must claim responsibility for our actions if our business good or bad. If it is not performing, we need to find a way to get it performing. If what we are doing is not working, we have to do more of what will, and change the strategy to suit. If we have the wrong team, we need to free them up and find more suitable opportunities.

It is you, as the business owner, that needs to be fully accountable for your actions – you wanted to be your own boss right? So it is important, when things are not going well, not to play the victim role and the blame game. This will take your eye off what you need to be doing to get back and stay on track, especially staying ahead of your competitors.

If we are blaming everyone and everything for our problems, it leaves no room to realise that maybe it is our fault and no one else's. Playing above the line in the space of victor Not victim, will be integral to you obtaining a stronger mindset for success.

I know I'm potentially making this sound all too easy, and you may be a little frustrated as a result. However, look at it like this – in hard times you are planting the seeds for future growth, and building the much-needed muscle to get you through other tough times.

So when things get easier, you will be primed and in the best position to capitalise on the good times ahead and hit your straps to prosper.

And remember, there is an excellent chance your competitors are not doing the hard work you are willing to do, so ultimately in time, this work will pay dividends in many different ways. Think of it like positioning yourself to get set up for downhill momentum, using less effort to get a much higher result.

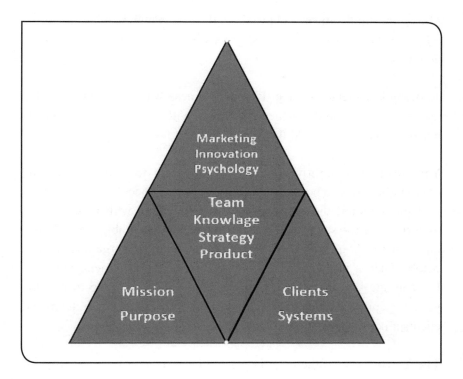

So, what is the mission for your business? Please understand I am not asking what is your expectations on the profit you will make today next week or at the end of the year.

No, I'm talking about the bigger reason you are getting out of bed in the morning with a spring in your step. Having a clearly defined mission should be the DNA of your company, as it is this statement that contains information like a map for your future. Guiding the team and your clients to know what the business stands for, and is all about.

Most importantly you must have the right energy behind it, as just words on paper that look cool or sound great will not get you the momentum you need.

This sends a clear message. If your business was the most respected by your people and partners, coupled with an admiration for its performance, what would that mean for you?

Your team will intuitively know the direction to improvement and continually strive to be the most admired by their peers. Moreover, they will aim to uphold the standards for the partnerships which are required to perpetuate the statement. This will equal an admirable performance due to the right attitudes and culture of the team and organisation as a whole. That is just my basic interpretation of the statement, however, I encourage you to look at it carefully and take the time to develop your mission and statement that underpins your organisation, team and clients alike.

The Team is one of the most important parts of your business. Even if you are a team of one, you still require a team to help run your business.

Putting the team together requires some real thought in and around your mission, the last thing you want is a team who are all the same as you, as this will more than likely be detrimental to the mission, in that everyone will want to do the same thing.

Having different skillsets and points of view in your team is important for getting strength and depth within the organisation. As mentioned, even if you are a team of one you will more than likely require the following team members like accountants, book-keepers, social media and website development people, marketing consultants, a performance coach and so on.

Knowing yourself is important, to know what additional resources are required to bolster the areas you are less skilled in, or have no intention of learning or doing.

Everyone has a genius inside, understanding that part, teasing it out and working to its strengths will create the most leverage for you and your business. Moreover, when you and your team are doing what is more enjoyable, life for everyone is a whole lot easier and way more productive.

There are many high-quality dynamic testing tools available. I have found them to be most comprehensive in understanding your strengths and weaknesses.

Having employees that are willing to sign on to your mission, that have the right skillset and a personality that truly complements yours and the rest of the team, is what you have to search for and find.

Don't Give Up

Your mind will want to quit long before your body is unable to perform the task. It is said that when we think we're done and have no more to give, it is possible we have only exerted one-half of what we are able to accomplish. I always like to draw on my 'real life' accounts as it gives me more clarity and strength when I'm in the trenches doing it tough.

I can recount an Ironman competition I competed in and won. It was certainly not that I possessed more skill than my competitors. In fact, I was in the bottom 50% of the team, who displayed some exceptional talent.

The one difference was I had a steadfast will to succeed and, importantly had trained hard to ignore the tricks my mind would undoubtedly play, in conjunction with the internal dialogue designed for self-protection and preservation, which, more often than not, becomes our biggest saboteur – those instinctive survival voices, telling you to slow down or stop, or that you have nothing to be ashamed of not finishing or coming last. That if you don't stop you may face some serious damage to your body and maybe unable to train ever again.

I needed to have already seen myself winning the event many times over; I had won in my mind long before I got out on the field. I had a strategy; I stayed focused on the outcome not how hard the training was. Giving thanks, and being grateful for winning, long before I did.

So how do we use the power of the knowledge to get momentum and stay in the Power Zone, requiring less effort to be propelled along?

Getting up at 5am religiously, exercising daily, being at peace with your thoughts and spending time getting clarity, and reading and educating yourself on business, and the power of the mind. Doing the One Percenters and the most important things first – note I said the most important, not the most exciting.

Leaders are the ones that set higher standards than anyone else, they get in and do what is required to get momentum going. Quite often the boring stuff first, then when things are moving along they can hand that over to the team to get leverage.

Then their skill and expertise come in to play to keep the momentum going. Skilled leaders and entrepreneurs understand how important it is to maintain the foot down hard on the gas, especially when things are going well.

While their competitors are resting, the best in the business are working smarter and more efficiently, resulting in exponential growth with far less effort. Always conscious of staying in the power zone and not settling for just 'good'.

A leader's job is to be of service and do the work that others not willing to do, to turn the hard grind from challenging situations around, adding a sense of excitement and creativity regarding what can be achieved.

Now, I need to clarify something – there is a big difference between a leader and a manager. Not taking anything away from managers, they are leaders of sorts, while they are standing over the team and ensuring compliance with the systems and procedures.

How do you know if you are leading or managing your tribe? If you can leave the environment, and the tribe are compelled to continue with the plan and stay true to the mission and vision without you being there, you are leading.

If the moment you stop supervising and enforcing compliance with the mission the team begins to wander off track and change the agenda to suit themselves, you may be only managing.

Most importantly for you as the leader of your business, family, and friends, it is your job to empower others to be leaders as well. This is a true sign of a leader. This helps to allow you to quantum leap ahead of your competitors giving a much sort after lead that generates confidence and clarity for the team moving forward.

How can you step up in an incremental way to improve as the leader in your business, family, health and mind every day?

Look for innovation that you can apply in thinking, encouraging, and doing what's required to engage and solidify your leadership credentials. This will be your Power Zone, ensuring your business is in a more commanding position.

Being a leader of your life will require you to take more uncomfortable positions, as you are continually needed to expand, grow, and become more. This is where mental strength comes in, and your fitness and prowess as a dynamic business owner, ready for whatever comes your way.

Marketing

A predictable thing happens if we don't market our business – NOTHING.

Marketing is the first domino that must fall before anything else is in order to get your story out there and tell it in a way that **Stands Out** from your competitors, to a crowd that is willing to listen to what you have to say.

One of the MOST crucial skills you need to master as a business owner/ entrepreneur is how to market successfully in order to position you and your business.

A word of warning – marketing is a highly potent multifaceted tool, so be sure that you can back up and deliver on all of your promises, as you can blow yourself up quick smart if you cannot. Trust is one of the first things your potential clients are looking for, and if they don't trust you, you're in for an uphill battle. You have to be prepared to give maximum value and then some. Don't be concerned about offering a portion of your best to give away before you have the right to ask for anything in return.

We are in a day and age of being overwhelmed in a world highly saturated by information, bombarding us from every angle. TV, radio, the internet, social media, signage, direct mail, phone calls, emails, text messages, cold calling, spam, the list goes on.

You are only consciously aware of a small portion of the messaging that happening to you, but behind the scenes your brain is clogging up with the stuff and becoming desensitised to taking action.

Cutting through all of the clutter needs a different approach, not simply a 'bells and whistles' one.

All too often I see businesses spending money hand over fist on marketing that is just vanilla, average, and the same as everybody else is doing. Disappointed business owners wait impatiently for some action from the hard earnt dollars spent, getting little or no return.

Technology has reached a point where it can target your exact 'Rock Star Client' and put your highly-appealing bait right in front of a potential prospect. But this style of marketing is often not used to its full potential, as most people don't pay close attention to the right placement and message that the audience wants and needs. Finding out what the market or niche wants **and giving it to them in abundance** is the simplest and most efficient way of getting significant results.

Surveying your niche and asking the right questions will set you up with the appropriate information required to build a thriving business. This has been a fundamental key in starting my businesses and getting others' back on track – including my own.

First, you need to be sure there is a high want and/or need for what you are offering, as this is often a reason for failure, or a struggle to get enough clients. You may have fallen in love with your product or business but your target audience has not. Meaning you're in for some interesting times ahead.

So, the first question you need to ask your demographical market either when starting a new business, or trying to grow or recover and existing one is: IS THEIR STILL A HIGH WANT OR NEED FOR WHAT I AM PROVIDING? If there is not, you could be in for a very uncomfortable ride: one I would not recommend taking.

If this is the case then consider your options carefully, as there may be an opportunity to reinvent your processes and intended audience, in changing the way you do business, requiring a case by case approach to finding an appropriate solution for your personal needs.

However, let's look at what we know about the marketplace to give us some clues on how to create the right process for getting our message to the market.

1. **The bait needs to be big enough and of the right type to get the attention of clients.** Give it your best effort so your bait stands out from all the others.

2. **Test the market on what they want, and what works.** Ask your potential clients what they want.

3. **Stack the value so high as to take your opposition off the table.** Be prepared to give extra away with your initial offer.

4. **Change the buying criteria in the way your clients think about buying your product or service.** Educate the marketplace on why they should buy your product over anyone else's.

5. **Have a strong guarantee that is incredibly compelling.** Trust is the biggest hurdle to overcome in today's unreliable market.

6. **Build your database, as it is one of the most valuable assets to your business.** Your private group of potential buyers as your captive audience.

7. **Create your expert persona.** Be the educator of your market and in doing become the trusted authority.

So, let's look at these in more detail. Having the right bait can sound condescending, however, it does not necessary have to be cold-hearted and deceptive. Yes, you are doing your best to influence potential clients to take action, but that's because you are offering an excellent product, service, and advice, so you owe it to them and your business.

Taking away the possibility of your would-be client getting inferior service and products from a competitor with less than ethical intentions is your responsibility. Understand the bait is the extension of your business, your unique message, plus your offer to the market. Think about this carefully as Mediocre and Generic will not cut it anymore, in this ever-changing competitive market.

We are talking about a high quality product (not necessarily the best product) it must have plenty of sizzle – sell the benefits of your offering here.

You must have a Compelling Headline, Sub Heading, and well-written copy explaining how their life will be better, how their problem will go away, or how you will make them feel fantastic about themselves. Importantly, you must boost their confidence, so their fears and frustrations subside.

Paint the picture, so they feel like your service and product is the obvious one to choose. As it could make them the most money, stop their stress, feed their hunger and make them look cool in front of their friends, family, and peers. Whatever the problem, you must find a solution.

So how do you know their fears, frustrations, and challenges? Test small and often, using different bait, and monitor the results very carefully. 'What you think' does not matter – there is only the Market.

Everybody has a tipping point, the time at which the offer is just too compelling to say no to. Stacking the value so that your initial offer has an accompaniment of other valuable benefits attached is key to widening your net, and increasing your take up.

Now I'm not talking about discount here. Add-on extras can be cheap for you to give, but never underestimate the perceived additional benefit to your client – it all adds up in their mind.

Every opportunity you get, via all forms of media, you need to tell your story – why are you different? What is your X factor? How will your offering benefit your client in multiple ways? "We are good honest people, and we offer an excellent product" will not cut it anymore, even if you are the best. Everyone else is telling the same story.

One way of standing out from the crowd is to have a Highly Compelling Guarantee – one that stops them dead in their tracks. Here are some examples,

"100% Satisfaction Guarantee or Your Money Back."

"10 Year Warranty on Parts and Labour."

"We will fix it in 24 hours, or we will pay you $1000.00." – even if it is Christmas day

You get the point, but make sure you can back your promise and that it fits within the mathematics of the sale. It must be VERY compelling, though, or your prospects won't take action.

Your Private Audience

One of the most undervalued parts of your business is your database. For me, it is the most valuable part, because, without the ability to market to your list at will, you are at the mercy of the highly expensive magazines, publications or online advertising.

With a broadly segmented database, you have your own captive audience, and you can control when and how compelling opportunities get offered to them. The main cost is the acquisition of the lead, after that it is very cost-viable to continue building a relationship, nurturing and, importantly, capturing sales from your tribe.

One of the best ways to nurture and build a trusting relationship with your tribe is to educate them on their interested subject. Become the maven of your industry, the Trusted Adviser, that the people look up to get the right unbiased advice.

You don't want to sell to them as they will quickly lose interest and remove themselves from the group. I find a combination of informational videos, newsletters, and direct mail gives the best response and conversion.

With this mix of media, you can offer plenty of high-quality educational content, about your products, services and team, explaining the benefits and points of difference adding to you position as the obvious choice.

This one thing alone has been responsible for getting more clients into my business than anything else; it is super-powerful and gives you credibility you can't buy, and your competitors will not do it.

Now that you have Rubber to the Road and good momentum, you are ready to take it to the next level, feel confident you have all the equipment to get there.

CHAPTER 10

TAKING IT TO THE NEXT LEVEL

CHAPTER 10

TAKING IT TO THE NEXT LEVEL

People often ask me "What is the Next Level and how will I know when I get there?"

I can't answer that question for you, as only you know where your Next Level is. It is different for all of us.

I can tell you this; it is not an elitist's view on getting further ahead than the next person, especially if it is to their detriment. It is a measurement of your personal efforts in fulfilling your life's mission in a creative way.

This is not a comparison with anyone else's life, as comparing yourself to others can be detrimental to your own advancement and growth.

The Next Level is a state of never-ending improvement in many areas of your life, as there is always the Next Level, like a never-ending ascending staircase to the stars. One only your imagination knows the boundaries of.

Before anyone else will follow and trust you, first you need to trust yourself, because if you don't trust yourself, and in your ability to achieve results, neither will anyone else.

People will know if you don't trust yourself they can hear it, see it, and feel it. Like anything you want to improve it needs to be measured accurately.

> " Imagine if you could have an amazing prosperous life long experience by simply initiating the same unwavering faith, attention and energy you give to **FEAR** every day. "
>
> GLEN MICHAELIDES

Commit to your mission and have the guts to do what is necessary to go out and achieve it as you may just learn one idea could be a real game changer for you.

For me the longest journey has been the one from my head to my heart as for me and you this is where you will find your true genius.

The natural forces of the Universe will meet you halfway, you need to be seeking searching, trusting and perfecting your next level to find the meeting point or you may just miss it.

Use your new found abilities to strengthen the voices of others in need as challenges come to all of us when we think we don't need them.

When things get tough and don't go your way, and they will, you have the ability to stay graceful as your internal world will be so well crafted and amazing, even if the outer world appears miserable and challenging.

If everything was an opportunity happening for us, would you act with less resistance and learn to ask new questions? As if you believed it is for your own good what could you create from the difficult situation that you could do right now to help yourself and many others?

Dismiss the Nay-sayers

Build yourself on being braver stronger and smarter every day, knowing that you are building on progress over trying to be perfect.

If you are threatening the masses this is real evidence that you are on the right track, love your family and friends as not everyone will understand you, but choose your peer group wisely.

The Power of 4

So let's look at the different areas of our life, break them down, and get an understanding on how we can quantify the improvement in these regions.

Firstly, it is important to be conscious as to where you are spending most of your time; this exercise can be a little confronting for some. As mastering one area at the expense of another is going to unbalance your circle of life and slow you down.

If you look at the following diagrams, to gain maximum power speed and efficiency of **The Power of 4 Wheel** needs to be balanced. If it is not, your life is out of balance and your more than likely in for a bumpy ride.

Note that in the following examples, showing 'out of balance', and 'in balance', if you are not putting the required amount of effort in all sections of the Power of 4, you will be out of balance and lose power.

Be aware that sometimes your unobtainable expectations can hold you back as whenever you feel a lack of achievement in one area you tend to try and overachieve in another to fill the void. This will get you further out of balance.

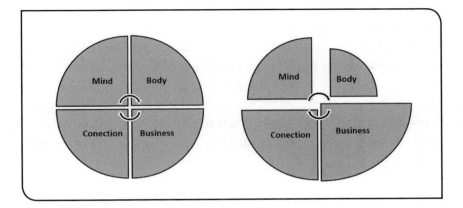

- So think carefully about this, because if your **Business** is doing well at the expense of your Family life you will be out of balance.

- Having the best **Family life** with no money to provide for them will eventually cause stress and also get you out of balance.

- If you lose your **Health** through poor diet, lack of exercise, stress and overworking on your business you will be out of balance.

- Take care of your **Mind** if you want it to take care of you – not spending time on your thinking and thoughts will have an effect on your subconscious and you will be out of balance.

Maintaining Balance may require you to think differently than currently. If you think you are in balance right now, that's great. However, I've found the effort towards balance is a never-ending one as everything is always changing and needing constant attention.

Maintaining the quest for balance will require you to understand yourself. You have to have the courage to bring the real you forward, as there is unbelievable joy and excitement in moving toward your worthy ideal.

If I had a time machine and go back to my younger years what would I tell myself? I would be very tempted to reveal all of the secrets I now know. I wouldn't though, as I would not want to risk learning the lessons from all of the hardship, good times, failures, wins, success and craziness that have happened for me over that time.

Don't beat yourself up about past failures, silly mistakes, stupid things you may have done or said to people. It has all been for your own good in getting you to this point and ready for the next level. In a small amount of time people forget and forgive so don't keep punishing yourself for past indiscretions. Align your energy, nourish yourself from the inside out.

Use this book, the tools, strategies, psychology and hindsight as a springboard for your Next Level. Because going to your Next Level is only one way, moving forward not backward and making a promise to yourself to do so regardless.

There is more to it than just getting through your day and doing what's in front of you. It's about a measured approach to steadily improving in all areas. The Power of 4 is a guide to help you to reach your Next Levels in all four areas consistently and sustainably.

How do you measure and maintain your promise to balance out your life and keep the Power of 4 balance operating a high level?

Firstly, you need to answer the following questions before you move forward.

- What do you want?

- Why do you want it?

- By what Specific Action?

- By what Strategy?

- In what Time Frame?

The Power of 4 Mind Body Connection and Business

- Mind

- Body

- Connection

- Business

What are the four most important things you need to do every day in order to get to the Next Level?

I want you to do this exercise

Write down four of the most important things you need to complete in each area of the Power of 4 every day in order to strive for better balance in each quadrant.

Let me give you some examples

1.   Mind: you may have spent time getting clarity on your goals, been conscious of the quality of your thoughts, meditated and connected spiritualty

2.   Body: you may have exercised correctly, eaten essential foods for your health, drunk the right amount of water and rested adequately.

3.   Connection: you may have spent time building strong relationships, said the special things to loved ones, took the time to understand another's model of the world, helped someone in need.

4.   Business: you may have learnt a new marketing concept, took time out to train the team, analysed the profit and loss, and developed a new sales strategy.

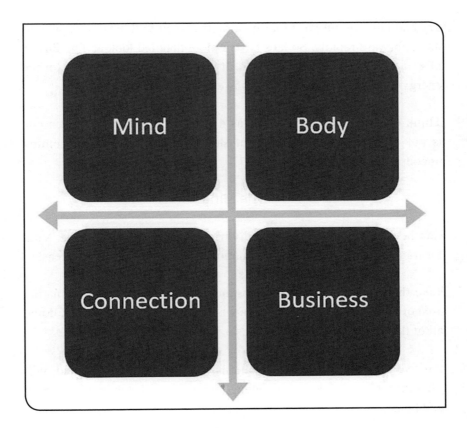

Score yourself out of 4 for each section in the previous diagram. If you are achieving all of your targets each day you will have received a total of 16 points.

This is your outcome to achieve for yourself as you will be setting the criteria of your Power of 4 to improve on.

Understand that continual improvements in each sector will get you to your Next Level much sooner.

Try and balance out your four quadrants so you will have the power to move forward rapidly. So let's have a more detailed look at **The Power of 4** and why each is so important. If you are lacking in one sector the energy leakage will reduce your power.

Think of the 4 areas of mastery as 4 wheels on a vehicle if even one is out of balance you will feel it slowing you down and becoming uncomfortable and clunky.

The Mind

Can be seen as the computer and wiring system of your vehicle. Vital for transferring energy and information to all of the important areas.

Take the time to study and understand the mind, as it is a fascinating area of learning. Your subconscious is the default programming, doing all of the driving behind the scenes, so you need to look after it.

Positive affirmations and incantations, said continually out loud, will filter through and if done with enough intensity will etch into your mind and body.

Meditation is an excellent way to rebalance your brain and clear your thoughts. I have also gained much clarity and forward momentum from the process of NLP and Hypnosis. Like movies in your mind you get the choice as to which ones you play swapping out what's not serving you anymore and relacing with your ideal version.

Spend time finding ten things every day that you are grateful for right now, this one thing on its own will set off a chain reaction that will simply amaze you.

The Body

Is the main structure of your vehicle. If you're not looking after your body, it will also have an effect on your mind, connection with others and your business.

Your health is number one, without it there is no Next Level. I love this quote from an unknown source "If you don't look after your body, where are you going to live?" Sums it up nicely I think. Being an entrepreneur demands a lot of energy, willpower alone won't get you through.

Eating the right foods is extremely important for most people and the addition of the exercise will have a positive effect. So, more often than not, the medicine or the poison is in the food we eat and the exercise we chose to do or neglect.

If you are looking to improve your Power of 4 don't try and all of the sudden to never eat unhealthy foods, as that won't be sustainable for most long-term. Try instead introducing more vegetables, clean water and slowly balancing out the good to bad ratio.

By introducing more, you will find there will be less room for the not so good stuff, and you won't feel like you are missing out. Your body will adjust and crave less of the bad food.

The same principals exist with exercise, from ridiculous over-the-top programs that will make the average person want to quit in the first couple of days, to boring mundane, repetitive cardio that drives you insane.

Your Next Level is *your* Next Level; no one else's so if you are currently not exercising at all, start by going for a ten-minute walk and build it up from there to 30 min plus.

For the more advanced at exercise, keep challenging yourself to hit your targets as consistency is the key. It is said that 30 minutes a day can have a profound effect in staving off disease and improving mindset dramatically, to name a few of the many benefits from exercise. Don't overdo it though, as your body needs all-important recovery time.

Connection

This is the contact and grip needed to get movement with your vehicle. It is critical for all of us to be at the highest level here, as it's required to keep us, excited, growing, sharing and consistently learning.

When life gets challenging, to have a shoulder to lean on makes the world of difference to our ability to handle tough situations for us and others.

We are built to be together, creating memories with your loved ones is the number one.

Connect with the universal energy. Draw this in to raise your energy to a higher vibration. This is a divine energy source when connected to can charge you and your business in a phenomenal way.

Connecting with others in need is extremely gratifying, coaching and training people to release their maximum potential is one of the most exciting assignments on earth.

To think you can make a significant difference in someone's life, so they can switch their thinking to an abundant mindset, helping them create their own compelling outcomes. And to change the world for others in our own special way, will cause your world to change for you in a special way.

Business

This is the fuel for your vehicle get clear, find what you are extremely passionate about doing, use the information in this book, be fully committed, and take action to doing the necessary work.

Business is number one in giving you the much needed revenue and potential tax savings to give the propulsion your vehicle needs.

Success in business is directly in proportion to the amount of value you are prepared to give, so spend the time to forge strong relationships pay it forward and it will come back tenfold.

Learn to embrace the challenging times, and know that you have powerful support in staying on purpose – surround yourself with people who have your best interests at heart, as you prepare to climb to your Next Level.

As at the top of the mountain lies the bottom of the next, as it is not the luckiest that can reach new heights more the ones that practice being lucky every day.

Getting Back on Top

The pages of this book contain real-life content for you to really learn to uncap your unlimited power. We are surrounded by unlimited energy everywhere and don't generally give much thought to where it comes from when we turn on a light switch, or go to start our car in the morning.

One of my most important parts of my day and my set up for success is generated by my early morning meditation sessions. So I wanted to share with you some important tools.

Everyone has their own religious beliefs and I respect that, use your own version if you will, and feel free to modify to what is my secret weapon above anything else.

- Get yourself in a quiet, peaceful comfortable location – for me it is near the water

- I ask for permission from God and the divine to bring down the powerful healing energy

- I ask that my subconscious use the energy to heal and repair my nervous system, immune system, and eliminate everything that is not required

- Relax, eyes closed, palms up and with anticipation see the powerful energy coming in from the heavens through the top of your head and travelling down through your body

- As it travels through feel the smooth soothing energy, see it repairing and nurturing whatever is required and solving any problems you may have

- Feel the energy traveling down through your body taking anything unwanted away, see the energy going through your body and down through your feet to the core of the earth. Watch it travelling all the way back in a split second through your feet, body and back through the top of your head into the universe in a cycling motion. With each new pass comes more nurturing energy

- While this is happening think of five things you are grateful for and really put some emotion behind it

- Keep the energy cycling through and think forward to three things you want to achieve it can be anything at all, see it in your mind's eye with clarity as if you are already living it. Feel what it would feel like to have achieved those outcomes and hear yourself being congratulated for getting to your Next Level

- Know that you can bring in this powerful energy anytime you want as it is limited only by your imagination.

Engaging Your Force Field

I encourage you to take five minutes out a couple of times during your day to reset your energy flow. When you feel yourself getting caught up in the busyness of business, stop and take some time out to engage your force field.

Imaging the powerful rays of the sun coming down to from an impenetrable triangle large enough to fit yourself and your love ones into. See yourself stepping into the triangle as only the powerful energy of good can enter nothing bad can get in. It is impenetrable to everything else and will giving you much needed support no matter how challenging things get.

See this energy overwhelming and nurturing the inside of triangle so that all inside get to experience this warming glow.

This is a place where you feel joy and are grateful for the important things in your life. A place that you can go to anytime you or loved ones need sanctuary and protection.

The power of spending the time and meditating on your triangle will give you a sense of confidence, strength and clarity to gracefully move through your day.

Getting Results

The chapters you have read in this book are not just theory, as the strategies tools and psychology I have shared, have made the big difference in my businesses, especially to get back on top when all seemed hopeless.

The road to recovery was not an easy one and did take a lot of discipline. I wish I could say it was as easy as snapping my fingers and it all just happened.

One thing I'm most proud of is that all of my staff were treated with dignity and respect, I never missed a payroll, and I fulfilled all of my obligations, even if it meant selling off all the things I had worked so hard for over many years.

I needed to start from the beginning, as hard as that was, and not cut any corners if I was to thrive long term.

I made the decision to rebuild and put the momentum behind it.

I developed the energy by having a big enough 'why' reconnecting with my mission and that of the company, and I enlisted help from experts in their fields and drew on their experience in creating the plan.

I took the time to build a world-class team who complemented my strengths and weaknesses. Who, importantly, understood and were on-board with mine and the company's mission and vision.

I structured the systems to support the staff with accurate recordings and measurements of our performance. I factored in remuneration and consequences, allowing the realisation of the business and their full potential and capacity.

I learnt and understood intimately all of the figures, including the profit and loss, balance sheet, operating cash and assets.

I surveyed my clients and found out their fears, frustrations, and what they wanted, to develop and craft a marketing message and strategies that exactly matched what our prospects were looking for.

I understood the maths in giving away a profit upfront, for a profit I would not have gotten if I did not, providing added value by stacking the benefits to our clients making our offer incredibly compelling.

I trained the sales staff to be educators and givers of high value, giving them the tools in their toolbox to take away reasons for not buying, allowing them to convert at a much higher percentage.

We developed strong guarantees that gave peace of mind taking away more objections upfront, and adding incentives for our client's regular contact and nurturing to increase transactions.

We put in place ten separate referral strategies that involved free gifts for the referrer, loyalty cards and affiliate commissions and so on.

We held our prices and profit margin by giving more value than our competitors in the form of extended warranties added bonuses better quality products and additional service.

We understood and acknowledged their lifetime value and rewarded them accordingly with birthday gifts, VIP service, and made them feel special.

All of that, in turn, provided massive leverage for the business and staff alike and actually turned the company around.

So if you are starting out in business or you are in a challenging situation take solace in the pages of this book and people who have proven up the formulas for success.

Know that it is possible to have it all without sacrificing, becoming out of balance and the next statistic.

Most importantly I did not do it alone I had the support of friends, family, and mentors all helping me through the journey.

Especially one great friend and mentor that – without her wisdom and guidance – I would not have made it through the dark valley to emerge out the other side stronger, wiser and more fulfilled.

Her marvellous gift was helping me create space from the inside, eradicating all of the poison, fear, scarcity, anger and frustration that had filled up my internal fortress.

The creating of room that allowed me to refill my heart and soul with the energy, love, compassion and wisdom required to continue to fulfil my mission in life.

And for that, I will be forever grateful.

These and many more experiences have given me the energy, wisdom, and hindsight to give back to those in need.

I have owned and run many businesses over the years and gained much needed skills from the variety. I am clear and concise on what I am put here to do as my mission as the founder of "The Titans Academy" is "To Evolve People and Business in Transformational Change and Leadership." Creating a movement through empowering special people just like you, to step up as leaders and change the world in your own special way.

Whether you need help to get to your next level, or are ready to step up and become the next Titan willing to go the extra mile for people in need, we are ready and waiting with open arms to help you get to your next level.

www.TheTitansAcademy.com.au

AUTHOR'S FINAL WORD

Everything is different now.

I look at the world differently now, almost as looking through a different set of eyes, that see differently. I hear sounds I had long forgotten, and feel feelings that had been dead in me for the longest time.

Even if I wanted to go back I could not, as the opening from where I came into this new world has disappeared. There is a feeling a loss and sadness for the people, places and business I have left behind. But there is a knowingness of an inbuilt force inside that is always encouraging and driving me to push on, and move forward when the time is right. And leave the comfortable places I have only just begun to enjoy.

My vision is that there is also a force within you; maybe you are already in tune with it. For others you can sense it but are not ready to act on it until it is overwhelming.

Stepping up to the Next Level can be a lonely place at times, reaching the summit a height where most are not willing to climb to share in your achievements.

At this place you breathe a different type of air and speak an alternative language making it difficult to explain at times. Understand you are built this way, and you will have the strength to make it to the Next Level.

At the Next Level you catch your breath for just long enough to gaze out over the horizon to see an even bigger summit in the distance. Gathering support from others on the same journey you know and understand what's required and that the next adventure is just around the corner.

Taking a big breath, you step off into the unknown prepare for the interesting times you will face through the valley, to once again to find your Next Level.

The fact that you think it is possible it's because it is, and I believe in your courage as an entrepreneur and a leader to go out and get it.

You are the master of your world and energy!

ABOUT THE AUTHOR

Glen Michaelides Author Profile

Glen is first and foremost a Family man and enjoys nothing more than sharing fun times with his loving family.

Glen is an author, entrepreneur, public speaker, and real estate investor.

Having started his first business at the age of ten, Glen was destined to be a successful businessman. Despite the many challenges of business, Glen's ability to leverage growth in his company's has seen outstanding results in cases in excess of $14 million.

In addition to his personal business success, he has managed and grown several multi-million-dollar businesses in a diverse range of sectors, including health and fitness, share trading, and real estate.

Leveraging his business insight and his knowledge of the stock market, he has been involved in trading complex stock transactions. Additionally, Glen has used his skills in business to buy, build, and sell real estate properties worth millions of dollars.

Including the thousands of individuals Glen has helped throughout his career, he has worked with many organisations including BHP, Alcoa, Rio Tinto, HWE, Leighton's, FMG, police organisations, fire and emergency organisations, Power companies, and several gymnasium franchises.

In his spare time, he enjoys owning and driving exotic cars as well as participating in motorsports and water ski competitions. A winner of an Ironman competition, Glen has also competed in martial arts events and has trained with champion power lifters and body builders.

Glen also enjoys meeting celebrities from around the world. And he supports a variety of children's charities.

Apart from Glens achievements that he believes are possible for anyone, his mission is to create positive lasting change by strengthening the voice in others, so they can live without fear and go on to make their own positive impact on the world.

RESOURCE SECTION

RESOURCE SECTION

Discover How You Can enjoy Success in your Business and Lifestyle sooner with My Private Personal Mentoring.

You may now be well aware of sabotaging factors that may be holding you back from achieving the things you want.

Learn How You Can Have X-Ray Vision Avoiding **the Fatal Mistakes Business Owners Make.**

You see, over the past 20 years I've been responsible for making a big difference in the lives of my clients by providing them with the right strategies, tools, and psychology so they can un-tap their full potential and get the success they deserve.

And what I've realised is that most people don't have a clear direction and outcome for designing their Ultimate business and lifestyle.

I'll share with you… how to lay down your ultimate blueprint so you can take charge of your lifestyle and Business right now.

Remember, the name of the game is to enjoy financial and lifestyle freedom sooner. But this won't happen successfully if you just keep going on the way you are now and don't take action today!

I need to show you the next step, which is **How to Double or Even Triple Your Profits… While Working Less, And Enjoying the Things You Want!**

Clients pay me to get them results that are far from average.

So if you want **more profits in your business while working less, and enjoying the things you want**, then Talk to Glen about VIP personal mentoring.

glen@thetitansacademy.com.au

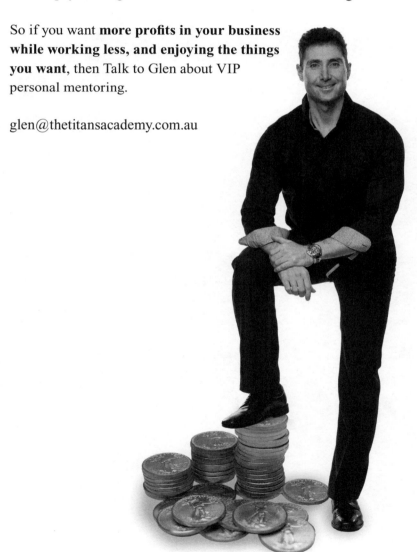